# Love Like Christ

1 Corinthians 13:4-7
"Love is patient, love is kind… it does not envy, it does not boast, it is not proud."

The foundation of a godly relationship isn't attraction or compatibility — it's Christlike love.

COUPLES' FAITH JOURNAL

A 52-WEEK JOURNEY TO GROW IN FAITH, LOVE, AND PURPOSE TOGETHER

AUTHOR: STEPHANIE M. MORELAND

"Though one may be overpowered, two can defend themselves. A cord of three strands is not quickly broken." – Ecclesiastes 4:12

🌿 DEDICATION

FOR EVERY COUPLE SEEKING TO LOVE GOD FIRST AND ONE ANOTHER FAITHFULLY — MAY THIS JOURNAL GUIDE YOU INTO A DEEPER, UNSHAKABLE BOND IN CHRIST.

💬 Introduction from the Author

When I began writing this journal, my heart was focused on one simple hope — to help couples draw closer to God and each other, one week at a time. This journal was born out of prayer, reflection, and love for my daughter and her boyfriend, a couple that I want to draw closer in their walk with god.. I wanted them — and others — to have a gentle guide that makes faith feel real, personal, and shared.

Life can pull us in so many directions. It's easy to let prayer, Scripture, and time with God drift into the background. But when two people invite God into the center of their relationship, something sacred happens — their love takes on strength, purpose, and peace that nothing else can give.

This journal isn't about perfection or checking boxes. It's about slowing down together, listening for God's voice, and learning how to build a relationship grounded in His Word. Some weeks will speak directly to your heart, others might challenge you to see things differently. Take it at your own pace. Let God meet you where you are.

My prayer is that as you journey through these pages, you'll begin to see how faith transforms everything — the way you love, forgive, speak, and grow. And as you walk together, may you always remember: a cord of three strands — you, your partner, and God — cannot be broken.

With love and blessings,
 Stephanie M. Moreland

# Table of Contents

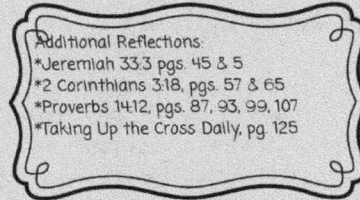

I...

# How to Use this Journal

⬜ Dear Reader,

This journal was created to help couples grow closer to each other and to God — to build a foundation of faith that lasts through every season. There is no "perfect" way to use it, only a prayerful and intentional one. Below are a few notes to help you along the way:

## 1. Use Your Bible Alongside This Journal

It is highly recommended that you keep a Bible nearby as you work through each week. Reading Scripture directly from God's Word allows the Holy Spirit to speak to you personally — beyond what's written on these pages. Verses may take on new meaning when you see them in context, and you may be led to explore other passages that deepen your understanding. God often reveals something fresh when we open His Word ourselves.

## 2. About the Writing Space

As the author, I purposely did not leave space under every question or statement. Some prompts are meant to spark reflection in your heart or conversation with your partner, not always to be written down. For those of you, like me, who have larger handwriting or want to write more, I recommend keeping a separate journal nearby for deeper notes or extended reflections. The important part is your growth, not how much you write.

## 3. You Don't Have to Follow the Weeks in Order

Even though the journal is organized by weeks, life doesn't always move in perfect sequence — and that's okay. Feel free to skip around. Some lessons may speak more directly to your current season or challenges. It would be wonderful if each couple could complete one lesson per week, but if you miss a week, don't feel discouraged. God meets you wherever you are.

## 4. Enjoy the Journey

This is not just a workbook — it's a shared journey of discovery, prayer, and growth. Enjoy the process of learning together and communicating openly. Celebrate what God is doing in your relationship. As you study, pray, and reflect, may you both experience a deeper connection with each other and with the One who holds you together — the strand of three cords that cannot be broken.

"Though one may be overpowered, two can defend themselves. A cord of three strands is not quickly broken." — Ecclesiastes 4:12

✦ Author's Note:
There is no grade, no timeline, and no "right" way to complete this journal. Simply invite God into your conversations, and He will do the rest.

# The 7 Foundation Prayers

1. Prayer of Surrender — Putting God First
"Lord, help us to put You above everything else in our lives — above our plans, our feelings, and even each other. Teach us to seek Your will first in every decision we make."

2. Prayer for Unity — Becoming One in Spirit
"Father, make us one as You and Jesus are one. Remove pride and selfishness that divide us, and teach us to walk together in love, patience, and peace."

3. Prayer for Guidance — Following God's Direction
"Holy Spirit, lead our steps. When we're unsure, remind us to pause, pray, and listen. Help us trust Your voice more than our own understanding."

4. Prayer for Purity — Living in Holiness
"Jesus, keep our hearts pure before You. Guard our thoughts, our words, and our actions so that everything we do honors You and reflects Your holiness."

5. Prayer for Faith — Trusting God in All Seasons
"Lord, strengthen our faith when life feels uncertain. Help us believe that You are working all things together for our good, even when we cannot see it."

6. Prayer for Love — Reflecting Christ in Our Relationship
"Teach us to love as You love — selflessly, forgivingly, and faithfully. Let our words and actions show others what it means to be rooted in Your love."

7. Prayer for Purpose — Serving God Together
"Father, reveal the purpose You have for us as a couple. Show us how we can serve others, bring glory to Your name, and build Your Kingdom together."


These prayers are the foundation of this journey. Return to them anytime you feel distant, uncertain, or in need of renewal — they are reminders that every strong relationship begins and ends with God.

# Putting God First

**SCRIPTURE FOCUS**

"But seek first his kingdom and his righteousness, and all these things will be given to you as well." — Matthew 6:33

**SHORT LESSON:**

A Christ-centered relationship begins with God at the very center. When we put God first above our own desires, above each other, and above the distractions of this world, we build a foundation that cannot be shaken. Many couples unintentionally make each other the center of life, expecting their partner to meet every need. But only God can truly fulfill us. When we seek Him first, everything else falls into place: stress lightens, peace grows, and love deepens.

**GUIDED PRAYER:**

Heavenly Father,
Teach us to put You above ourselves and above each other. Forgive us for the times we've placed our desires or relationship before You. Show us how to seek You first in everything—our choices, our words, our plans. Be the foundation of our love and guide
our steps.
In Jesus' Holy name, Amen.

**REFLECTION QUESTIONS::**

In what ways do we currently put our desires before God's will? Examples: skipping prayer, entertainment before Scripture, prioritizing each other's approval over God's Word.

How can we remind each other daily to keep God first? Do we pray together? Do we encourage each other spiritually?

What might change if we truly sought God first? Examples: less stress, more peace, fewer arguments, more trust in God.

**WEEKLY CHALLENGE**

Pray together every morning this week, even if it's just for one minute.

Daily Prompts

Day 1: Write down one area of your life where God is not first.

Day 2: Read Matthew 6:25-34. What does this passage teach about trusting God?

Day 3: Write a short prayer asking God to be first in your life.

Day 4: What priority most often replaces time with God?

Day 5: Create a simple "God-first" habit as a couple (example: pray before meals).

Day 6: Reflect: How might putting God first change how we treat each other?

# Prayer as a Couple

**SCRIPTURE FOCUS**

> "If two of you on earth agree about anything they ask for, it will be done for them by my Father in heaven. For where two or three gather in my name, there am I with them." — Matthew 18:19-20

**SHORT LESSON:**

Prayer is the heartbeat of the Christian life. When couples pray together, they invite God into the center of their relationship. Jesus promises that when two agree in prayer, God listens and responds. Prayer doesn't have to be long or fancy—it just needs to be sincere. Consistent prayer unites hearts, strengthens intimacy, and reminds us that God is the source of love and wisdom.

**GUIDED PRAYER:**

Lord Jesus,
Thank You for the gift of prayer. Teach us to come before You together with humility and faith. Remind us that You are with us when we pray. Unite our hearts in love, give us courage to pray consistently, and let our prayers strengthen our relationship.
In Jesus' Holy name, Amen.

**REFLECTION QUESTIONS:**

Do we pray together regularly, or mostly alone? Example: "We pray together daily" / "We rarely pray as a couple."

How do I feel when my partner prays for me? Examples: encouraged, supported, nervous, unsure.

What keeps us from praying together more often?

**WEEKLY CHALLENGE**

Pray together every morning this week, even if it's just for one minute.

Daily Prompts
Day 1: Write a short prayer for your partner..

Day 2: : Read Matthew 18:19-20. Do we believe Jesus is present when we pray? Yes/No.

Day 3: Pray for another couple you know. Write down their names.

Day 4: Thank God out loud for three things about your partner.

Day 5: Share one worry with each other and pray about it.

Day 6: Reflect: How did praying together make me feel this week?

# Hearing God's Voice

**WEEK 3**
**SCRIPTURE FOCUS**

"My sheep listen to my voice; I know them, and they follow me." — John 10:27

### SHORT LESSON:

God speaks today through His Word, through prayer, and through the Holy Spirit. Jesus said His sheep hear His voice—meaning that as believers, we can learn to recognize when He is leading us. For couples, listening for God's voice brings clarity to decisions and unity in direction. Sometimes God's voice is a quiet peace or conviction that aligns with Scripture. Listening requires slowing down, being still, and creating space for Him to speak.

### GUIDED PRAYER:

Heavenly Father,
Help us to recognize Your voice above all others. Teach us to listen carefully in prayer and in Your Word. Give us discernment as a couple to know when You are speaking, and courage to follow You faithfully.
In Jesus' Holy name, Amen.

### REFLECTION QUESTIONS:

Do we pause to listen for God after praying, or do we move on quickly? Yes or No

Have we felt God guiding us as a couple before? Examples: peace in a decision, conviction about a choice?

What can we do to seek God's voice more often? Examples: read Scripture aloud, sit quietly, journal thoughts, church

12

**WEEKLY CHALLENGE**

Continue to pray together every morning this week, even if it's just for one minute.

Daily Prompts
Day 1: Read John 10:27. Do I believe God wants to speak to us? Yes/No

Day 2: Write one way I've felt God guide me in the past..

Day 3: Sit in silence after prayer for 2 minutes. Write what I sensed. (Joy or gratitude, peace, calm, conviction that I should_____)

Day 4: Read Psalm 46:10. What does "Be still and know" mean for us?

Day 5: What competes most with God's voice in our lives? Ex: social media, job, entertainment, each other

Day 6: Share one verse that stood out this week and how it applies.

# The Holy Spirit's Guidance

## WEEK 4

### SCRIPTURE FOCUS

Since we live by the Spirit, let us keep in step with the Spirit." — Galatians 5:25

### SHORT LESSON:

The Holy Spirit is God's gift to every believer—our helper, teacher, and guide. For couples, walking in step with the Spirit means making decisions that honor God and turning away from anything that pulls us away from Him. The Spirit gives wisdom when we're unsure, conviction when we're drifting, and power when we're weak. He also produces fruit in us—love, joy, peace, patience, kindness, goodness, faithfulness, gentleness, and self-control. When a couple lives Spirit-led, their relationship reflects the heart of Jesus.

### GUIDED PRAYER:

Holy Spirit,
Guide our steps as a couple. Help us to walk in step with You daily. Show us what we should let go of and what we should embrace. Fill our relationship with Your fruit and help us to honor Christ in every decision.
In the power of the Holy Spirit, we pray. Amen.

### REFLECTION QUESTIONS:

Do we invite the Holy Spirit to guide our choices as a couple? (Yes/No)

What habits or activities might the Spirit be asking us to let go of? Examples: unhealthy entertainment, gossip, cursing, premarital sex

Which fruit of the Spirit do we need most in our relationship right now? Examples: patience, kindness, self-control. (see the lesson for more)

## WEEKLY CHALLENGE

Pray daily this week: "Holy Spirit, lead us today."

Daily Prompts
Day 1: Read Galatians 5:22-23. Which fruit of the Spirit do I see most in my partner?

Day 2: Write one habit we could change to better honor God. Example: Instead of sleeping in on Sundays, commit to worshiping with other believers and serving in community; stop cursing or negative talk, and replace it with words that encourage and build up; instead of scrolling on our phones before bed, we read one psalm or pray together.

Day 3: Ask the Spirit to convict us before speaking hurtfully. Did we notice it? Yes/No

Day 4: Pray for peace in a stressful situation. Did we feel it? (Yes/No)

Day 5: Write one way God reminded us of His Spirit's presence this week. Ex: Through answered prayer, through peace in stress, through conviction or guidance, through scripture or encouragement from others.

Day 6: Reflect: How could walking in the Spirit change our relationship? Ex: Holiness in daily life. → "The Spirit would convict us when we slip into sin or bad habits and help us live in a way that honors God together." Strength in trials. → "We would lean on God instead of stress, trusting Him instead of worrying."

# Guarding Words & Actions

### SCRIPTURE FOCUS

"Do not let any unwholesome talk come out of your mouths, but only what is helpful for building others up." — Ephesians 4:29

### SHORT LESSON:

Our words have power. They can build up or tear down. In relationships, words shape trust, safety, and love. Harsh words can leave deep wounds, but words of blessing bring life. God calls us to guard our tongues and choose speech that builds each other up. This includes our tone, our patience, and even how we speak about each other when apart. A Christ-centered couple speaks life and encouragement, using words to point each other back to Jesus.

### GUIDED PRAYER:

Our Most loving and sovereign God:
Set a guard over our mouths. Forgive us for careless or hurtful words. Help us to speak with love, encouragement, and truth.
May our words build up each other and honor You.
In your precious name, Jesus. Amen

### REFLECTION QUESTIONS:

Do we often speak before thinking? (Yes/No)

What words or tones hurt our relationship most? Examples: sarcasm, shouting, ignoring.

How can we speak more encouragement to each other this week? Examples: affirmations, gratitude, kindness.

Speak at least one word of blessing to your partner every day this week. EX: Encouragement → "You are a gift from God to me, and I'm grateful for your patience."Affirmation → "God has given you such wisdom, and I admire the way you handle challenges."Spiritual Blessing → "May the Lord give you peace today as you go into work."

Daily Prompts

Day 1: Write three kind words about your partner. Share one aloud.

Day 2: Read James 3:9-10. How can blessing and cursing come from the same mouth?

Day 3: Think of one phrase I should avoid saying. Write it and why.

Day 4: Share one encouraging Scripture with your partner today.

Day 5: Confess one careless word I said recently and ask forgiveness.

Day 6: Journal: How did speaking blessings this week affect our relationship?

# Trusting God in Stress & Worry

## WEEK 6

### SCRIPTURE FOCUS

"Do not be anxious about anything, but in every situation, by prayer and petition, with thanksgiving, present your requests to God. And the peace of God... will guard your hearts and your minds in Christ Jesus." — Philippians 4:6-7

### SHORT LESSON:

Worry is one of the biggest thieves of joy in relationships. Stress about money, health, or the future can cause tension and arguments. God calls us to bring our anxieties to Him in prayer instead of carrying them alone. He promises peace that surpasses understanding—a peace that unites and strengthens couples. When you face stress, pause together, pray, and surrender your concerns to God. Trusting Him brings peace where worry once ruled.

### GUIDED PRAYER:

Father, Your Word tells us to 'cast all our cares on You,' and that's what we do right now. We lay our worries before You. Help us to trust You with our needs and our future. Replace our stress with Your peace. Show us how to encourage one another to pray instead of panic. Remind us daily that You are faithful to provide. Our hope is in You alone.
In Christ Jesus' name we pray. Amen.

### REFLECTION QUESTIONS:

Do we talk to God about our worries together, or mostly to each other?

What is our biggest source of stress right now? Examples: finances, family, work.

How might trusting God change the way we handle stress? Examples: calmer, more patient, less arguing.

## WEEKLY CHALLENGE

Pray together whenever stress arises this week before discussing solutions

Daily Prompts

Day 1: Write one worry we will give to God today.

Day 2: Read Matthew 6:34. What does it mean not to worry about tomorrow?

Day 3: How does stress affects the way we treat each other?

Day 4: Share one answered prayer from the past as a reminder of God's faithfulness.

Day 5: Pray together about one financial or future concern. Example: "Father, You are our Provider and everything we have comes from You. We bring our financial worries to You today. Give us wisdom in how we spend and save, peace to trust You in times of lack, and faith to believe You will meet our needs. Help us honor You with our finances and remember that You are always faithful. In Jesus' name, Amen."

Day 6: Reflect: Did trusting God this week bring us more peace? (Yes/No)

# Obedience Over Comfort

## WEEK 7

### SCRIPTURE FOCUS

"Do not merely listen to the word, and so deceive yourselves. Do what it says." — James 1:22

### SHORT LESSON:

Faith isn't just about hearing God's Word—it's about living it out. As a couple, obedience may mean making choices that are difficult in the short term but bring blessing in the long run. Sometimes it's easier to do what feels comfortable than to do what honors God. But true love for God is shown in action. When you walk in obedience together, you will find strength, joy, and peace that surpass what comfort could ever give.

### GUIDED PRAYER:

Father God, show us the way we should go today.
Help us not to just hear Your Word but to obey it. Give us courage to make choices that honor You, even when it costs us something. Unite us in faith and action as we follow You together.
All praise and honor be to You, O Lord. Amen.

### REFLECTION QUESTIONS:

Do we sometimes know what God wants but delay in obeying? (Yes/No)

What area of our lives is God asking us to obey Him more fully? Examples: forgiveness, generosity, purity, attending church, secular things.

How does obedience show our love for God? Examples: trust, surrender, sacrifice.

**WEEKLY CHALLENGE**

Identify one area where God is calling you to obedience and take a step together this week. Examples of Obedience Steps for a Couple:

1. Church & Worship → "God is calling us to commit to attending church regularly. This week we will choose a service and go together."
2. Speech & Words → "God is convicting us about our language. This week we'll work on cutting back on cursing and replacing it with encouraging words."
3. Finances → "God is calling us to be generous. This week we will set aside part of our income to give or help someone in need."
4. Prayer Life → "God is urging us to be more consistent in prayer. This week we'll pray together every night before bed."
5. Purity → "God is calling us to set better boundaries in our physical relationship. This week we'll avoid situations where we are tempted."
6. Serving Others → "God is nudging us to serve. This week we'll volunteer one evening at the church food pantry."

Write your couple goal here:

Day 1: Read James 1:22. Do we practice what we hear? (Yes/No)

Day 2: Write one step of obedience you have been avoiding.

Day 3: Share one time obedience to God brought blessing.

Day 4: Pray for courage to obey in a current situation.

Day 5: Journal: How do I feel after obeying God quickly?

Day 6: Reflect: What step of obedience will we take this week?

# Reading the Bible as One

**SCRIPTURE FOCUS**

> "Your word is a lamp to my feet and a light to my path." — Psalm 119:105

### SHORT LESSON:

God's Word gives light, direction, and strength for daily life. As a couple, reading Scripture together strengthens your bond with each other and with God. You don't need to study for hours—even a short passage each day can shape your hearts. The Bible corrects, comforts, and equips us. When couples invite God's Word into their relationship, they learn to see life through His perspective and align their decisions with His truth.

### GUIDED PRAYER:

Dear Heavenly Father,
Thank You for the gift of Your Word. Help us to read it together faithfully. Open our eyes to see Your truth and teach us to apply it in our lives. May Scripture be the foundation of our relationship.
In the Lord's Almighty name, Amen.

### REFLECTION QUESTIONS:

Do we read the bible together regularly? (yes/no)

What usually keeps us from reading scripture? Examples: distraction, forgetting, busyness

How could we make scripture be a bigger part of our relationship/ Examples: reading before bedtime, reading before we start our workday, sending each other a scripture for the day.

## WEEKLY CHALLENGE

Read at least one passage of Scripture together every day this week.

Daily Prompts
Day 1: Read Psalm 119:105. What does it mean that God's Word is light?

Day 2: Share your favorite verse and why it speaks to you. Write it here.

Day 3: Journal one way Scripture encouraged and/or corrected you recently.

Day 4: Read one Psalm aloud. Which verse stood out to us?

Day 5: Write down one verse to memorize as a couple.

Day 6: Reflect: How did reading together affect our connection this week?

# Worship & Church Community

**WEEK 9**

**SCRIPTURE FOCUS**

**SHORT LESSON:**

We are not meant to live the Christian life alone. Worshiping God together, especially in community, strengthens faith and deepens love. Church isn't just a building—it's the family of God. Couples who make worship and fellowship a priority grow stronger roots in Christ. Worship is more than singing; it's a lifestyle of honoring God. Gathering with other believers keeps you accountable and reminds you that you're part of something bigger than yourselves.

**GUIDED PRAYER:**

Our Heavenly Father
Thank You for the gift of worship and community. Help us to make time for church and fellowship. Teach us to worship not just with words, but with our lives. Surround us with people who encourage us to grow closer to You. Thank you, Lord Jesus.
Amen.

**REFLECTION QUESTIONS:**

Do we regularly attend church together? (Yes/No)

What do we gain when we worship with other believers? Examples: encouragement, accountability, growth.

How can we bring more worship into our daily life? Examples: music, gratitude, prayer, join bible study.

**WEEKLY CHALLENGE**

Attend one worship service or Bible study together this week.

Daily Prompts
Day 1: Read Hebrews 10:24-25. Why is gathering important for believers?

Day 2: Journal: How do I feel after worshiping at church?

Day 3: Choose a worship song to listen to together. Reflect on the lyrics.

Day 4: Pray for your pastor or church leaders today.

Day 5: Write one way worship strengthens our relationship. Examples: Shifts Perspective → "Worship reminds us that God is greater than our problems, which takes pressure off our relationship." Deepens Love → "Singing and praying together fills my heart with gratitude for God and for my partner." Invites Peace → "Worship calms us after stress and brings peace into our home."

Day 6: Reflect: How can we make worship more consistent in our life? Examples: Schedule Worship → "Set aside Sunday mornings for church and protect that time, no matter what." Daily Music & Prayer → "Play worship music in the car or at home and sing or pray along together." Family Devotions → "Read a psalm out loud before dinner or bedtime as part of our routine." Community Involvement → "Join a small group or Bible study where worship is part of the rhythm." Personal Reminders → "Use reminders on our phones to pause once a day and thank God together."

# Confession & Repentance

## WEEK 10

### SCRIPTURE FOCUS

"If we confess our sins, he is faithful and just and will forgive us our sins and purify us from all unrighteousness." — 1 John 1:9

### SHORT LESSON:

Confession is not about shame—it's about freedom. God invites us to bring our sins into the light so He can forgive, heal, and restore. Repentance means turning away from sin and walking toward God. In relationships, confession builds honesty, and forgiveness builds trust. Couples who confess before God and repent together experience renewal. Grace is the soil where love grows.

### GUIDED PRAYER:

Father,
Thank You for Your mercy and forgiveness. Help us to confess our sins honestly and repent with sincere hearts. Teach us to show grace to each other when we fall short, just as You have shown us grace.
Amen.

### REFLECTION QUESTIONS:

Do we confess our struggles to God regularly? (Yes/No)

Why is repentance important for our relationship? Examples: healing, humility, restoration.

How can we extend grace to each other when one of us makes mistakes? Examples: forgiveness, patience, encouragement.

**WEEKLY CHALLENGE**

Confess one struggle to God this week and commit to turning away from it.

Daily Prompts
Day 1: Read 1 John 1:9. What does God promise when we confess?

Day 2: Write one area where I need God's forgiveness.

Day 3: Pray together for strength to repent from one habit.

Day 4: Share one past mistake God has forgiven to encourage each other.

Day 5: Reflect: How does it feel to be forgiven by God?

Day 6: Write a prayer of thanks for God's grace and mercy.

# Love as Christ Loved

## WEEK 11

### SCRIPTURE FOCUS

> "Love is patient, love is kind. It does not envy, it does not boast, it is not proud. Love never fails." — 1 Corinthians 13:4,8

### SHORT LESSON:

True love is not just feelings—it's a choice to act like Christ. His love is patient, kind, forgiving, and sacrificial. For couples, this means choosing to love when it's hard, when patience runs thin, or when selfishness tempts us. Love that reflects Christ transforms relationships. It teaches us to serve, to forgive, and to remain faithful even in challenges.

### GUIDED PRAYER:

Lord Jesus,
Teach us to love each other as You have loved us. Help us to show patience, kindness, and forgiveness. When we are weak, strengthen our love with Your Spirit. May our relationship reflect the love of Christ.
Amen.

### REFLECTION QUESTIONS:

Which quality of love (patience, kindness, forgiveness) do we need to grow in most?

How can we love each other better when we're stressed or tired?  Examples: patience, gentle words, listening.

What does it mean to love each other "as Christ loved us"?

## WEEKLY CHALLENGE

Choose one Christlike act of love each day (kind word, patience, forgiveness).

Day 1: Read 1 Corinthians 13:4-7. Which word stands out most?

Day 2: Write one way my partner shows love to me.

Day 3: Write one way I can love my partner better this week. With Words
→ "I can love my partner better by speaking encouragement instead of criticism when they feel stressed." With Actions → "I can love my partner better by doing one of their chores this week without being asked." With Time → "I can love my partner better by putting my phone away and giving them my full attention during dinner." With Patience → "I can love my partner better by being slow to anger and quick to listen." With Prayer → "I can love my partner better by praying for them out loud each night."

Day 4: Pray for strength to love with patience today.

Day 5: Journal how Christ's love has changed my life.

Day 6: Reflect: How did choosing to love change our week?

# Forgiveness in Relationships

## WEEK 12

### SCRIPTURE FOCUS

> "Be kind and compassionate to one another, forgiving each other, just as in Christ God forgave you." — Ephesians 4:32

### SHORT LESSON:

Every relationship requires forgiveness. Words are said, mistakes are made, and disappointments come. Forgiveness doesn't mean ignoring wrongs—it means choosing grace instead of bitterness. God forgave us fully through Christ, and He calls us to extend that same forgiveness. Forgiveness heals wounds and opens the door to restoration. Without it, resentment grows and love weakens. Couples who practice forgiveness live with freedom and peace.

### GUIDED PRAYER:

Our gracious Lord and Father,
Thank You for forgiving us in Christ. Help us to forgive quickly and fully, without holding grudges. Give us hearts of compassion and grace for each other. Restore what's broken and keep our love rooted in Your mercy.
Amen.

### REFLECTION QUESTIONS:

Do I find it easy or difficult to forgive my partner? Why?

How does holding onto unforgiveness affect our relationship?
Examples: distance, anger, bitterness.

What does forgiving "as Christ forgave us" look like in our relationship?

**WEEKLY CHALLENGE**

When hurt this week, choose forgiveness first. Pray together instead of holding resentment.

Daily Prompts

Day 1: Read Ephesians 4:32. How has God forgiven me personally?

Day 2: Write one moment where I needed forgiveness recently.

Day 3: Write one moment where I forgave my partner. How did it feel?

Day 4: Pray together for a forgiving heart.

Day 5: Journal: How does forgiveness bring peace?

Day 6: Reflect: Did I forgive quickly this week? (Yes/No)

# Encouragement & Support

## WEEK 13

### SCRIPTURE FOCUS

"Therefore encourage one another and build each other up, just as in fact you are doing." — 1 Thessalonians 5:11

### SHORT LESSON:

Encouragement is like oxygen for a relationship. Words of support lift us up, give hope, and remind us that we are not alone. God calls us to build each other up, not tear down. Encouragement can be as simple as a kind word, a prayer, or showing appreciation. Couples who regularly encourage each other create a safe and loving environment where both can grow.

### GUIDED PRAYER:

Dear Lord,
Teach us to be encouragers to one another. Help our words to bring life, not harm. Show us how to build each other up in faith, love, and hope. May encouragement become a daily habit in our relationship.
In your precious name we pray, Amen.

### REFLECTION QUESTIONS:

Do we encourage each other often, or do we focus more on criticism?

What kind of encouragement means the most to me? Examples: words, actions, prayers.

How can I encourage my partner more this week? If you are unsure, ask your partner.

**WEEKLY CHALLENGE**

Give your partner one word of encouragement every day this week.

Daily Prompts
Day 1: Write one encouraging word for my partner today

Day 2: Journal: How does encouragement make me feel?

Day 3: Share a Bible verse of encouragement with my partner. Write it here:

Day 4: Write one way my partner encourages me.

Day 5: Encourage my partner in something they are working on.

Day 6: Reflect: How did daily encouragement change our week?

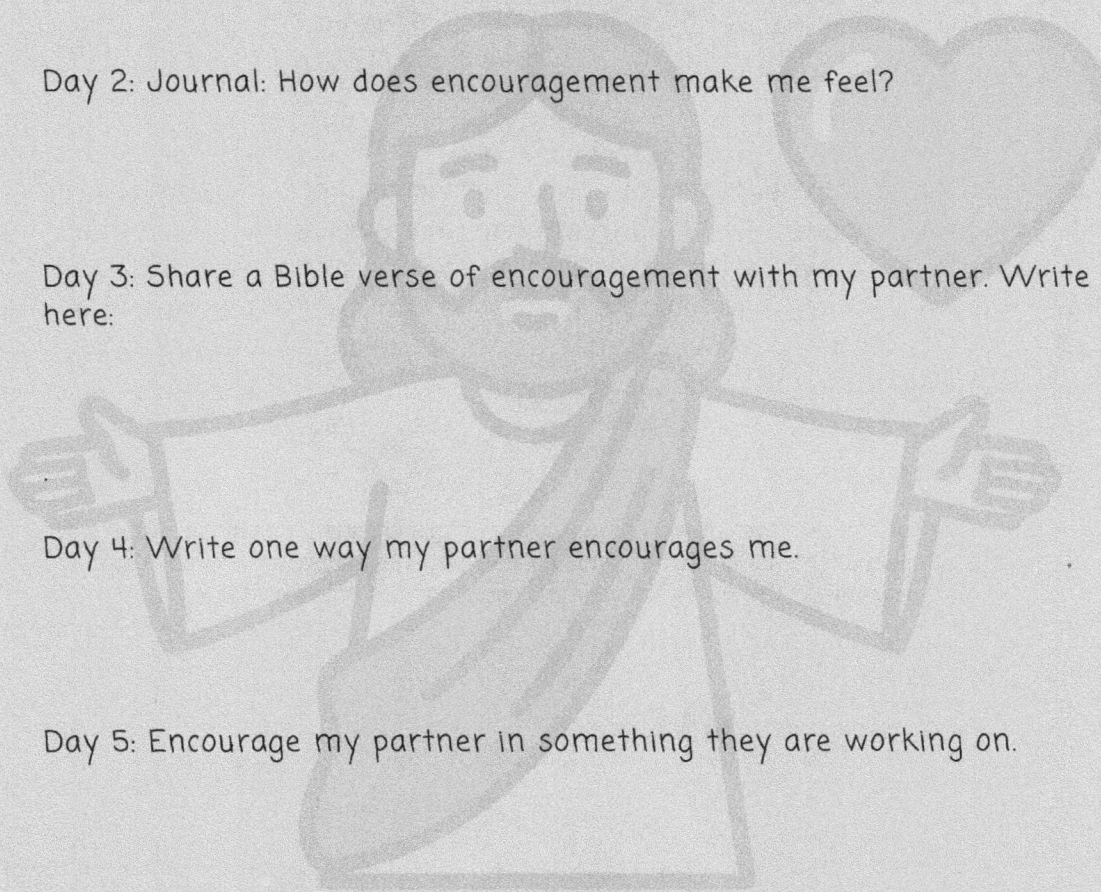

# *Patience with One Another*

## WEEK 14

### SCRIPTURE FOCUS

> "Be completely humble and gentle; be patient, bearing with one another in love."
> — Ephesians 4:2

### SHORT LESSON:

Patience is one of the greatest gifts you can give your partner. Love takes time, and people make mistakes. Impatience leads to frustration, sharp words, and division, but patience shows love, humility, and trust in God's timing. In relationships, patience means slowing down, listening, and choosing to respond with gentleness instead of anger. Just as God is patient with us, He calls us to be patient with one another, allowing love to grow in a safe and gracious space.

### GUIDED PRAYER:

Dear Heavenly Father,
Teach us to be patient with each other. Help us slow down, listen, and love with gentleness. Remind us of how patient You are with us and let that patience shape the way we treat each other. Thank you for your endless grace and mercies.
Amen.

### REFLECTION QUESTIONS:

When do I find it hardest to be patient with my partner?

How does God's patience toward me encourage me to be patient toward others?

What practical step could I take this week to show more patience? Examples: Pause Before Responding → "When I feel frustrated, I'll pause, take a breath, and pray before I answer." Listen Fully → "I'll let my partner finish speaking before I respond, even if I disagree." Slow Down Routines → "Instead of rushing, I'll allow extra time in the morning, so we're not stressed with each other."

**WEEKLY CHALLENGE**

Pause and pray before responding when you feel impatient this week.

Daily Prompts
Day 1: Read Ephesians 4:2. What does bearing with one another in love mean to us?

Day 2: Write about a time my partner showed me patience. How did it help me?

Day 3: Journal one area where I need to ask God for more patience.

Day 4: Thank God in prayer for His patience with me.

Day 5: Share one situation this week where I was able to practice patience.

Day 6: Reflect: How did showing patience affect our relationship this week?

# Humility & Selflessness

## WEEK 15

### SCRIPTURE FOCUS

"Do nothing out of selfish ambition or vain conceit. Rather, in humility value others above yourselves." — Philippians 2:3

### SHORT LESSON:

Selfishness destroys relationships, but humility strengthens them. Humility is not thinking less of yourself but thinking of your partner more often than yourself. It is choosing to serve, to listen, and to care even when it's inconvenient. Selflessness creates unity because both partners are looking out for the other's best interests. Just as Christ humbled Himself to serve us, couples are called to love through humility and selfless acts.

### GUIDED PRAYER:

Jesus,
Thank You for humbling Yourself to serve us. Teach us to put each other's needs above our own. Remove pride, selfishness, and stubbornness from our hearts. Help us to serve one another in love, reflecting Your example.
Amen.

### REFLECTION QUESTIONS:

Do I struggle more with pride, selfishness, or stubbornness?

What is one way I could serve my partner more this week?

How does humility make a relationship stronger?

## WEEKLY CHALLENGE

Perform one selfless act of love for your partner each day this week.          Example of Acts of Selfless Love:

Do a Chore They Dislike → Wash the dishes, fold laundry, or take out the trash before they ask.

Offer Encouraging Words → Send a thoughtful text in the middle of the day: "I'm thankful for you, and I'm praying for you today."

Give Up Something for Them → Let them choose the TV show, meal, or activity even if it's not your first choice.

Acts of Service → Fill up their car with gas, pack their lunch, or bring them a cup of coffee without being asked.

Gift of Time → Put aside your own hobby or work for an evening to do something meaningful with them.

Prayer → Pray out loud specifically for their needs and well-being.

Daily Prompts

Day 1: Read Philippians 2:3-4. What does valuing others above ourselves look like?

Day 2: Write one area where I often put myself first.

Day 3: Journal one moment when my partner put me first. How did it feel?

Day 4: Write down one way I could serve my partner today. Do it.

Day 5: Pray for humility and the strength to serve like Christ.

Day 6: Reflect: How did serving each other affect our connection this week?

Ask your partner, how can I serve you better? Make asking your partner this question a new Godly habit each week.

# Respect & Honor

## WEEK 16

### SCRIPTURE FOCUS

"Be devoted to one another in love. Honor one another above yourselves." —
Romans 12:10

### SHORT LESSON:

Respect is the soil where trust and love grow. To honor your partner means to treat them with dignity, kindness, and appreciation. Disrespect—whether in tone, words, or actions—tears at the foundation of love. God calls couples to honor one another as precious gifts, showing love not just in big moments but in daily interactions. Respect builds safety, and safety builds love.

### GUIDED PRAYER:

Father,
Help us to respect and honor each other daily. Guard our words and actions so they reflect kindness and appreciation. Teach us to see our partner as Your gift to us and treat them with love and dignity.
Amen.

### REFLECTION QUESTIONS:

Do my words and actions always show respect to my partner? (Yes/No)

What makes me feel most respected in this relationship?

How can I show more honor to my partner in daily life?

## WEEKLY CHALLENGE

Make a list of five ways you can show respect and honor to your partner. Do one each day this week.

Daily Prompts
Day 1: Read Romans 12:10. What does honoring my partner mean to me?

Day 2: Write one way my partner shows me respect.

Day 3: Write one way I sometimes fail to show respect. Pray for change.

Day 4: Encourage my partner with words of honor today.

Day 5: Journal how respect impacts the strength of our relationship.

Day 6: Reflect: How did showing honor affect my partner this week?

# WEEK 17
## SCRIPTURE FOCUS

> "Everyone should be quick to listen, slow to speak and slow to become angry."
> — James 1:19

## SHORT LESSON:

Conflict is inevitable in any relationship, but how you handle it can either strengthen or damage your love. God's Word calls us to listen more than we speak, to control anger, and to seek peace. Arguments handled with prayer and humility become opportunities for growth. When couples let God lead in moments of tension, they learn patience, forgiveness, and love that goes deeper than disagreement.

## GUIDED PRAYER:

Our Father who art in Heaven, Hallowed be thy Name.
Help us to handle conflict in ways that honor You. Teach us to listen with patience, speak with kindness, and forgive quickly. Replace anger with gentleness and pride with humility. Guide us to seek peace in every disagreement.
Amen.

## REFLECTION QUESTIONS:

Do we usually listen to understand, or just to reply?

How can we keep anger from controlling our words and actions?

What step could we take to resolve conflict in healthier ways?
 Examples: Pray First → "Pause to pray together before continuing an argument."
Listen to Understand → "Take turns sharing feelings without interrupting."
Use Gentle Words → "Speak calmly instead of raising our voices."
Take a Break → "Step away for 10 minutes if emotions get too high, then come back to talk.
"Seek God's Word → "Read a verse on patience or forgiveness together before deciding how to move forward."

## WEEKLY CHALLENGE

When conflict arises this week, pause to pray together before continuing the discussion.

Daily Prompts
Day 1: Read James 1:19. Which part do I struggle with most: listening, speaking, or anger?

Day 2: Journal about the last argument we had. What could I have done differently?

Day 3: Write one prayer asking God to help us in conflict.

Day 4: Think of a time we handled conflict well. What made it different?

Day 5: Apologize to my partner for one harsh word or action this week.

Day 6: Reflect: How did inviting God into conflict affect our relationship?

# Intimacy & Purity

## WEEK 18

### SCRIPTURE FOCUS

> "Marriage should be honored by all, and the marriage bed kept pure, for God will judge the adulterer and all the sexually immoral." — Hebrews 13:4

### SHORT LESSON:

God created intimacy as a beautiful gift for couples. It is more than physical—it is emotional, spiritual, and relational. Purity means honoring God's design for intimacy and protecting your relationship from temptation. For couples preparing for marriage, this means setting boundaries and keeping Christ at the center. For married couples, it means cherishing intimacy as an act of love, faithfulness, and unity. Intimacy without God leads to emptiness; intimacy with God's blessing brings fulfillment.

### GUIDED PRAYER:

Father,
Thank You for the gift of intimacy. Help us to honor You in this area of our relationship. Teach us to keep our love pure and holy, protecting each other and glorifying You in our choices.
Amen

### REFLECTION QUESTIONS:

How do we view intimacy in light of God's Word?

Are there boundaries we need to set or strengthen to protect purity?

How can we honor God with our bodies and our love for each other?

## WEEKLY CHALLENGE

Have an open, honest, and prayerful conversation about intimacy and purity this week.

Daily Prompts
Day 1: Read Hebrews 13:4. What does purity mean in our relationship?

Day 2: Journal one way intimacy strengthens our bond beyond the physical.

Day 3: Write about one boundary that helps us stay pure.

Day 4: Pray together for protection from temptation.

Day 5: Write one way intimacy is a reflection of trust and love.

Day 6: Reflect: How did focusing on intimacy God's way affect us this week?

God's Design for Intimacy

Intimacy is one of God's most beautiful gifts to couples. It is far more than physical — it is emotional, spiritual, and relational. When experienced God's way, intimacy becomes a powerful bond that strengthens love, builds trust, and reflects Christ's covenant with His people.

## 🌿 Key Truths from Scripture

Intimacy is Holy.  God created intimacy to be enjoyed within marriage as a holy and sacred act. "Marriage should be honored by all, and the marriage bed kept pure." — Hebrews 13:4

Intimacy Unites.  Intimacy is about unity, not just desire. It draws a couple together in deep connection.  "The two will become one flesh." — Genesis 2:24

Intimacy Reflects God's Love.  True intimacy reflects Christ's sacrificial love —selfless, patient, and faithful. "Husbands, love your wives, just as Christ loved the church and gave himself up for her." — Ephesians 5:25

## 🌿 Why God's Way Matters

Protects the relationship from temptation.
Builds a foundation of trust and respect.
Deepens spiritual connection, not just physical.
Turns love into worship when it honors God.

## 🌿 A Closing Prayer

"Dear God: Thank You for the gift of intimacy. Help us to honor You with our bodies, our thoughts, and our choices. Teach us to cherish each other, keeping our love pure, faithful, and centered in You.  Amen."

# Jeremiah 33:3

Call to me and I will answer you and tell you great and unserachable things you do not know.

When Jeremiah was imprisoned in a dark cell, God didn't say, "Fix your situation" or "Figure it out yourself." He said, "CALL TO ME." Even in chains, Jeremiah could do that. So can we. When life closes in whether it is worry, grief, illness, pain or confusion, we are never powerless. We can always call on our Heavenly Father. He promises not just to listen, but to answer.

Sometimes our answer is peace in the storm. Sometimes it's direction we didn't expect. Sometimes is it just assurance that we are not alone.

Matthew 28:20
And surely I am with you always, to the very end of the age.

# Building Trust & Faithfulness

## WEEK 19

### SCRIPTURE FOCUS

"The Lord detests lying lips, but he delights in people who are trustworthy." — Proverbs 12:22

### SHORT LESSON:

Trust is the foundation of any relationship. Without it, love feels insecure and unstable. God calls His children to truth and faithfulness because these reflect His own character. In relationships, trust is built through honesty, consistency, and faithfulness—keeping your word and guarding your heart against temptation. Couples who live truthfully and honor their promises reflect God's faithfulness to the world.

### GUIDED PRAYER:

Lord,
Teach us to be people of truth and faithfulness. Strengthen our honesty with each other, protect us from temptation, and help us to be trustworthy in every word and action.
Amen.

### REFLECTION QUESTIONS:

Do I always speak truthfully with my partner? (Yes/No)

What helps me feel most secure and trusting in this relationship?

How does God's faithfulness encourage me to stay faithful?

## WEEKLY CHALLENGE

This week, commit to total honesty and keep every promise you make. In fact, make a promise to your partner to start the week and keep that promise.

DAILY PROMPTS
Day 1: Read Proverbs 12:22. Why does God delight in truth?

Day 2: Journal one way my partner has shown faithfulness.

Day 3: Write about a time when trust was broken and how it was restored.

Day 4: Share one area where I can be more consistent in keeping my word.

Day 5: Pray for protection against anything that could harm our trust.

Day 6: Reflect: How has trust strengthened our love?

# Preparing for Commitment
## (Engagement & Covenant Love)

**WEEK 20**

**SCRIPTURE FOCUS**

"Though one may be overpowered, two can defend themselves. A cord of three strands is not quickly broken." — Ecclesiastes 4:12

**SHORT LESSON:**

Commitment is more than a feeling—it is a covenant, a sacred promise. Engagement and marriage are not just about two people but about inviting God into the center of the relationship. A cord of three strands—God, husband, and wife—is strong and enduring. Preparing for commitment means seeking God's will, setting Christ as the foundation, and embracing marriage as a lifelong covenant of love and faithfulness.

**GUIDED PRAYER:**

Dear Heavenly Father,
As we consider commitment, remind us that marriage is holy and sacred. Help us prepare with wisdom, purity, and prayer. Teach us to place You at the center, making our love strong and enduring. Bless us, dear Lord, as we strive to please you and follow your word.
Amen

**REFLECTION QUESTIONS:**

Do we see commitment as a promise to each other and to God? (Yes/No)

What steps can we take now to prepare for a strong, God-centered marriage?

How does including God in our commitment make it different from the world's view?

## WEEKLY CHALLENGE

Pray daily for God's guidance in your relationship's future and potential covenant.

Daily Prompts

Day 1: Read Ecclesiastes 4:12. Why is a "cord of three strands" unbreakable?

Day 2: Journal one quality I value in my partner that prepares us for covenant love.

Day 3: Write a prayer asking God to guide our future together.

Day 4: Discuss what covenant love means to us.

Day 5: Share one area we need to strengthen before marriage.

Day 6: Reflect: How does preparing with God give me peace about the future?

## God's Design for Commitment

Commitment in relationships is not only a promise between two people — it is also a sacred covenant with God. The world sees commitment as conditional, based on feelings or circumstances. But God's Word calls couples to a deeper, lasting bond rooted in faithfulness, sacrifice, and love that mirrors Christ's love for His church.

### ✄ Key Truths from Scripture

Commitment Is Covenant, Not Contract
"What God has joined together, let no one separate." — Mark 10:9
 → A covenant is unbreakable because it is sealed by God Himself.
Commitment Requires Preparation
"Unless the Lord builds the house, the builders labor in vain." — Psalm 127:1
 → Couples must prepare for marriage by inviting God into every area of their lives.
Commitment Honors God
"So they are no longer two, but one flesh." — Matthew 19:6
 → True commitment reflects the unity God designed from creation.

### ✄ Reflection Prompts for Couples

Do we see commitment as a promise only to each other, or also to God? Why does that matter?

What steps can we take now to prepare for a strong, God-centered marriage?
(Examples: praying daily together, building financial unity, seeking premarital counseling, setting healthy boundaries.)

How does including God in our commitment make it different from the world's view of love and marriage?

### ✄ Practical Steps to Strengthen Commitment

Pray together daily for God's guidance in your relationship.

Surround yourselves with a community of faith-filled couples.

Discuss expectations openly and honestly.

Practice forgiveness quickly, keeping unity at the center.

Serve God together in your church or community.

### ✄ A Closing Prayer

"Lord, thank You for the gift of love and the sacred calling of commitment. Teach us to see our promise not only as a bond between us but as a covenant with You. Prepare us for a strong, God-centered marriage that reflects Christ's love to the world. Amen."

Prayer Based on Jeremiah 33:3
Call to me and I will answer you and tell you great and unsearchable things you do not know.'

Our Dear Lord God You are the creator of the universe and everything in it. That includes my partner and me. As we seek to grow in faith as a couple, please hear our prayer.,

Your Word promises that when we call to You, You will answer us and reveal great and hidden things that we cannot see on our own. Today we come before You with an open heart, calling on Your name. We admit that our understanding is limited, and we cannot see the whole picture of our lives, but You know all things.

Lord, speak to us in the quiet places of our soul. Show us the things we do not yet understand—the wisdom we need for today, the direction for tomorrow, and the peace that only You can give. Help us to trust that Your answers will come in Your perfect timing and in ways that are greater than we can imagine.

When we feel uncertain, remind us that You are the God of mysteries revealed, the God who hears, and the God who answers. We ask You to guide our steps, open our eyes to Your truth, and deepen our faith so that we may walk in confidence, not in our own knowledge, but in Yours.

Thank You, Lord, for inviting us to call on You, and for the assurance that You hear our prayers. We wait with expectation for the wonderful things You will reveal.
In Jesus' name, Amen.

# A Cord of Three Strands

## WEEK 21
## SCRIPTURE FOCUS

"Unless the Lord builds the house, the builders labor in vain."
— Psalm 127:1

**SHORT LESSON:**
Every relationship is built on something—desire, convenience, or love. But a lasting marriage must be built on Christ. When God is at the center, the relationship becomes a cord of three strands that cannot be broken. Without Him, even strong love will struggle under the pressures of life. Couples who build on God's Word, prayer, and His presence lay a foundation that lasts forever.

**GUIDED PRAYER:**
Lord,
Be the builder of our relationship. Teach us to weave You into every part of our love. Strengthen our bond with You as the unbreakable strand that keeps us together.
Amen.

**REFLECTION QUESTIONS:**

What is our relationship currently built on—ourselves, or God?

How can we strengthen the "third strand" of God in our love?

What happens if a couple leaves God out of their foundation?

## WEEKLY CHALLENGE

Commit to reading one Scripture together daily as part of your foundation.

Daily Prompts
Day 1: Read Psalm 127:1. Why must God build the house?

Day 2: Journal one way we've seen God strengthen us already.

Day 3: Write one weakness we need God to hold together.

Day 4: Pray for God to be the center of our relationship.

Day 5: Discuss how prayer and Scripture can become part of our daily routine.

Day 6: Reflect: Do I see God as the third strand in our relationship? Why/why not?

# God's Design for Marriage

## WEEK 22

### SCRIPTURE FOCUS

> "So they are no longer two, but one flesh. Therefore what God has joined together, let no one separate." — Matthew 19:6

### SHORT LESSON:

Marriage is God's design, created from the very beginning. It is not simply a contract, but a covenant between man, woman, and God. Becoming "one flesh" means unity in body, heart, and spirit. Marriage is meant to reflect Christ's love for the church—faithful, sacrificial, and everlasting. Understanding God's design helps couples prepare not for a temporary commitment, but for a lifelong journey of love and service.

### GUIDED PRAYER:

Father,
Thank You for creating marriage. Teach us to see it as holy and sacred, a reflection of Your love. Prepare us to enter into marriage with wisdom, faith, and joy.
Amen.

### REFLECTION QUESTIONS:

Do we see marriage as a contract or a covenant with God?

How does the idea of "one flesh" change how I see love and unity?

What can we do now to prepare for marriage God's way?

# WEEKLY CHALLENGE

Study one Bible passage about marriage together (Genesis 2, Ephesians 5, Matthew 19).

Daily Prompts
Day 1: Read Matthew 19:6. What does it mean to become "one flesh"?

Day 2: Journal one thing that excites me about God's design for marriage.

Day 3: Write a prayer asking God to prepare us for His covenant.

Day 4: Share one area of marriage that feels intimidating or challenging.

Day 5: Pray for wisdom in preparing for marriage.

Day 6: Reflect: How does God's design for marriage give me peace?

## 📖 God's Covenant & Preparing for Marriage

Marriage was never meant to be a human contract — it is a holy covenant designed and initiated by God Himself. A contract is based on mutual benefit and can be broken; a covenant is sealed by love, sacrifice, and divine promise. When a couple invites God into their relationship, they are no longer just making a commitment to each other — they are entering into a sacred partnership with Him at the center.

## 🌿 What Is a Covenant?

A Covenant Is Binding: It reflects God's unchanging faithfulness. "I will betroth you to me forever." — Hosea 2:19
A Covenant Is Sacrificial: It requires humility and surrender — putting the other's needs before your own.
A Covenant Is Spiritual: It joins hearts, minds, and spirits under God's authority.
In a covenant, both partners say not just "I love you" but "I choose to love you — before God — for life."

## 🌿 Preparing for a God-Centered Marriage

Pursue God First
 → Grow your personal relationship with Christ before focusing on your partner.
Pray Together Regularly
 → Make prayer the foundation of every major decision.
Build on God's Word
 → Study passages about love, humility, forgiveness, and covenant (Ephesians 5, 1 Corinthians 13, Matthew 19).
Seek Wise Counsel
 → Surround yourselves with married mentors or attend premarital counseling through your church.
Practice Purity & Boundaries
 → Honor God with your bodies and decisions. Purity builds trust and spiritual strength.
Serve Together
 → Serving others teaches teamwork, humility, and shared purpose.

## 🌿 A Covenant Prayer

Our Heavenly Father,
 Thank You for designing marriage as a covenant that mirrors Your love for Your people. Teach us to prepare our hearts, not just our plans. Make us faithful, pure, and humble. Help our love to be rooted in You — a love that keeps its promises and endures every season. In Jesus' name, Amen.

More in Depth with 2 Corinthians 3:18:

"And we all, who with unveiled faces contemplate the Lord's glory, are being transformed into his image with ever-increasing glory, which comes from the Lord, who is the Spirit."

## Context
In this chapter, Paul is contrasting the old covenant (the Law given through Moses) with the new covenant in Christ. When Moses came down from Mount Sinai, his face shone with God's glory, but the people couldn't look at it directly, so he wore a veil (Exodus 34:29-35). Paul explains that under the new covenant, through Christ, the veil is removed. We can come openly before God.

## Meaning
1. "With unveiled faces-Because of Jesus, nothing separates us from God's presence. We can approach Him freely, without fear or barriers.
2. "Contemplate the Lord's glory"-Believers reflect on, look toward, and even mirror the glory of Christ. By focusing on Him, we absorb His character and presence.
3. "Being transformed into his image" The Christian life is a process of transformation. We become more like Jesus—not instantly, but gradually.
4. "With ever-increasing glory" (or "from glory to glory")-This describes spiritual growth. As we walk with Christ, God changes us step by step, continually shaping us into His likeness.
5. "Which comes from the Lord, who is the Spirit"- his transformation is not self-made. It is the work of the Holy Spirit in us.

## Application
- This verse reminds us that the Christian life is not about rules but about relationship—living with open access to God through Christ.
- Transformation happens as we spend time in God's presence, worshiping, reading His Word, and letting His Spirit work in us.
- It gives us hope: no matter how far we feel from Christ's likeness, He is continually shaping us into His image.

✦ In short: 2 Corinthians 3:18 teaches that, because of Jesus, we can see God's glory clearly and be transformed by the Spirit into Christ's likeness—growing more radiant in Him day by day.

continued on page 65

# Serving One Another

## WEEK 23

### SCRIPTURE FOCUS

"The Son of Man did not come to be served, but to serve, and to give his life as a ransom for many." — Mark 10:45

### SHORT LESSON:

Jesus showed the ultimate example of service by giving His life. In relationships, love grows when both partners serve each other with humility and joy. Serving is not just doing chores—it's looking for ways to bless, encourage, and support one another. A serving heart makes love stronger because it shifts the focus from self to the other person.

### GUIDED PRAYER:

Lord Jesus,
Thank You for serving us with Your life. Teach us to serve
each other with love, humility, and joy. May our acts of service
reflect Your heart.
Amen.

### REFLECTION QUESTIONS:

Do I usually look for ways to serve, or to be served?

What act of service means the most to me?

How can I serve my partner in a new way this week?

## WEEKLY CHALLENGE

Each day, find one intentional way to serve your partner.     Example Acts of Service
1. Do a Chore for Them → "I'll fold their laundry or clean the kitchen so they can rest."
2. Encourage Them → "Send a text during the day to remind them I'm praying for them."
3. Acts of Care → "Make their morning coffee or pack their lunch without being asked."
4. Support Their Burden → "Take over one of their tasks for the day so they can relax."
5. Offer Prayer → "Pray out loud for something that's been stressing them."
6. Gesture → "Leave a handwritten note or Bible verse where they'll find it."
7. Be Present → "Pause what I'm doing to truly listen when they need to talk"


Daily Prompts

Day 1: Read Mark 10:45. What does Jesus teach us about serving?


Day 2: Journal one way my partner has served me recently.


Day 3: Write one act of service I can do today. Do it.


Day 4: Pray to thank God for my partner's willingness to serve.


Day 5: Share how serving each other made us feel this week.


Day 6: Reflect: How does service strengthen our love?

# Unity in Decision Making

## WEEK 24

### SCRIPTURE FOCUS

"Can two walk together unless they are agreed?" — Amos 3:3

### SHORT LESSON:

Unity is essential in relationships, especially when making decisions. Disunity causes conflict, stress, and confusion. God calls couples to seek His will and to agree together before moving forward. Unity doesn't mean one person always gets their way—it means listening, praying, and making choices together. When both seek God's direction, unity flows naturally.

### GUIDED PRAYER:

Dear God our Father,
Help us to be united in our decisions. Teach us to listen to each other and to You.
Give us wisdom and peace when choosing together.
All glory is given to you, Oh Lord. Amen.

### REFLECTION QUESTIONS:

Do we usually make decisions together, or separately?

How does praying together bring unity in decision-making?

What is one area we need to practice unity in right now?

## WEEKLY CHALLENGE

Pray over one big decision this week and make it together.

Daily Prompts
Day 1: Read Amos 3:3. Why is agreement important?

Day 2: Journal about a past decision where unity helped us.

Day 3: Write one decision we need to pray about right now.

Day 4: Pray for wisdom and unity in decision-making.

Day 5: Share how it feels when we're united in choices.

Day 6: Reflect: Did we invite God into our decisions this week?

# Financial Stewardship as a Couple

## WEEK 25
### SCRIPTURE FOCUS

"Honor the Lord with your wealth, with the first fruits of all your crops." — Proverbs 3:9

**SHORT LESSON:**

Money is one of the top causes of stress in relationships, but God has a plan for finances. He calls us to be wise stewards, to give generously, and to live free from greed. Couples who honor God with their finances build trust and peace. Financial unity means making a plan together, avoiding selfishness, and remembering that everything belongs to God.

**GUIDED PRAYER:**

Dear Gracious Lord,
Thank You for providing for us. Teach us to be wise stewards of the money You've given. Help us to honor You with our finances and to trust You as our provider.
Amen.

**REFLECTION QUESTIONS:**

Do we view money as ours, or as God's gift to manage?

How can we honor God with our finances this week?

What financial decision do we need to make together soon?

## WEEKLY CHALLENGE

This week, pray before making any purchase decisions.

Daily Prompts

Day 1: Read Proverbs 3:9-10. What does it mean to honor God with wealth?

Day 2: Write one financial blessing God has given us.

Day 3: Journal one area where we struggle with money.

Day 4: Share one way we could give or be generous this week.

Day 5: Pray for unity in how we handle finances.

Day 6: Reflect: Did honoring God in finances bring peace?

## 💲 Financial Stewardship as a Couple

Money can build or break relationships — but when handled God's way, it becomes a tool for peace, unity, and generosity. God doesn't just call us to manage money; He calls us to honor Him with it. Financial stewardship is not about control — it's about trust. As a couple, learning to see finances through a biblical lens brings freedom, not fear.

### 🌿 God's Perspective on Money

**God Owns Everything**
"The earth is the Lord's, and everything in it." — Psalm 24:1   → What we have isn't truly ours; it's entrusted to us to manage wisely.

**Give God First Place**
"Honor the Lord with your wealth, with the first fruits of all your crops." — Proverbs 3:9 → Tithing and generosity show gratitude and trust in God's provision.

**Avoid the Trap of Worry**
"Seek first his kingdom and his righteousness, and all these things will be given to you as well." — Matthew 6:33→ When we put God first, we no longer chase security — we rest in His care.

### 🌿 Practical Steps for Financial Unity

- Create a simple monthly budget together and pray over it.
- Tithe or give generously to a church or ministry that aligns with your faith.
- Set shared goals: saving, giving, and reducing debt as a team.
- Be transparent — no secrets about spending or accounts.
- Thank God regularly for His provision, no matter how small.

### 🌿 A Couple's Prayer

Dear Heavenly Father,
Thank You for providing for us in every way. Help us to see money as a tool for Your glory, not a source of stress or division. Teach us to be generous, wise, and faithful stewards of all You've entrusted to us. Unite us in our financial decisions and give us peace as we trust You to meet our every need.  Amen.

continued from page 57

Beholding Together — A Reflection on 2 Corinthians 3:18

"But we all, with open face beholding as in a glass the glory of the Lord, are changed into the same image from glory to glory, even as by the Spirit of the Lord."
— 2 Corinthians 3:18

When two hearts walk with God together, something sacred happens — their love becomes a mirror reflecting His glory. In this verse, Paul reminds us that as we behold the Lord, we are transformed into His likeness. This transformation is not a one-time change, but a continual process — from glory to glory — a journey that deepens over time.

As a couple, your relationship can be a living reflection of that transformation. The more you both fix your eyes on Christ, the more you begin to see His character shaping your patience, your forgiveness, your kindness, and your unity.

Let this verse remind you that the goal of your love is not perfection, but progress — becoming more like Jesus together, one step and one season at a time. The Spirit of the Lord is your guide and your helper in every moment, gently shaping your hearts to reflect His image in how you love each other.

# Hospitality & Serving Together

## WEEK 26

### SCRIPTURE FOCUS

"Offer hospitality to one another without grumbling." — 1 Peter 4:9

### SHORT LESSON:

Couples who serve together grow together. Hospitality means opening your home, your time, and your heart to others. It's about reflecting Christ's love in practical ways—sharing meals, listening, helping, and caring. Serving side by side strengthens unity and deepens purpose. Hospitality done in joy, not obligation, creates a home where others see Jesus.

### GUIDED PRAYER:

Dear Gracious and Almighty God,
Teach us to be hospitable and generous with our time and home. Help us serve side by side, reflecting Your love to others. Use our relationship to bless those around us.
Amen.

### REFLECTION QUESTIONS:

Do we practice hospitality joyfully, or with hesitation?

How can we serve others together this month?

How does serving side by side strengthen our relationship?

## WEEKLY CHALLENGE

Host one person, couple, or family this week with joy and prayer.

Daily Prompts
Day 1: Read 1 Peter 4:9. Why does God value hospitality?

Day 2: Journal about a time we were blessed by someone else's hospitality.

Day 3: Write one idea for how we can serve together this month.

Day 4: Pray for someone who needs encouragement this week.

Day 5: Share how it felt to serve someone as a couple.

Day 6: Reflect: How did serving together change our relationship?

# Pursuing Dreams Together

## WEEK 27

### SCRIPTURE FOCUS

"Take delight in the Lord, and he will give you the desires of your heart." — Psalm 37:4

### SHORT LESSON:

God gives each of us dreams, talents, and passions. As a couple, pursuing dreams together means supporting each other's callings and inviting God to guide them. Some dreams may change over time, but when rooted in Christ, they become opportunities to serve Him and others. Encourage one another, dream together, and trust that God will shape your desires to align with His will.

### GUIDED PRAYER:

Father God, Maker of the Universe and everything in it,
Thank You for giving us dreams and desires. Help us support one another and seek Your will above all. Guide our steps as we pursue what honors You.
All creation bows before you and we lift up our voices to join the chorus of praise. Amen.

### REFLECTION QUESTIONS:

What dream or goal has God placed in my heart?

Share a dream of yours with each other. How can I support my partner's dreams more fully?

How do we make sure our dreams align with God's will?

## WEEKLY CHALLENGE

Set aside time this week to talk about your dreams and pray over them together.

Daily Prompts
Day 1: Read Psalm 37:4. What does it mean to delight in the Lord first?

Day 2: Journal one dream I want to pursue with God's help.

Day 3: Write how my partner encourages me in my dreams.

Day 4: Pray together for God's direction over one dream.

Day 5: Share how it feels when my partner supports my goals.

Day 6: Reflect: How do shared dreams strengthen unity?

# Preparing for Parenthood (Even Before Children)

## WEEK 28

### SCRIPTURE FOCUS

"Start children off on the way they should go, and even when they are old they will not turn from it." — Proverbs 22:6

### SHORT LESSON:

Parenthood is a sacred calling, even for those not yet parents. Preparing now means praying for future children, learning to model faith, and setting spiritual foundations in your home. Children learn by watching, so the best preparation is living faithfully as a couple. Whether or not children are part of your future, the principle remains—create a legacy of faith that blesses the next generation.

### GUIDED PRAYER:

Lord,
We pray for the next generation, whether children You may give us or others we will influence. Help us prepare by living faithfully now. Teach us to be examples of Your love and truth.
Amen.

### REFLECTION QUESTIONS:

What values do we want to pass to future children or the next generation?

How can we prepare our home to be a place of faith and love?

Why is it important to pray for future children, even now?

## WEEKLY CHALLENGE

Pray daily this week for the children you may one day raise or influence.

Daily Prompts
Day 1: Read Proverbs 22:6. Why is early training so important?

Day 2: Journal what kind of example I want to be for future children.

Day 3: Write one value I want to build into our family.

Day 4: Pray for wisdom as future parents or mentors.

Day 5: Share how I see my partner as a future parent.

Day 6: Reflect: How does preparing now affect our relationship?

# Balancing Work & Relationship

## WEEK 29

### SCRIPTURE FOCUS

"Whatever you do, work at it with all your heart, as working for the Lord." — Colossians 3:23

### SHORT LESSON:

Work is a gift from God, but it can easily consume too much of our lives. A healthy relationship requires balance between work, rest, and love. God calls us to work diligently, but also to prioritize time for Him and for each other. Couples who balance work and relationship create rhythms that honor God, provide for needs, and nurture love.

### GUIDED PRAYER:

Lord,
Thank You for the work You've given us. Teach us to balance work and love, giving our best to You and to each other. Protect us from stress and overwork, and help us to rest in You.
Amen.

### REFLECTION QUESTIONS:

Do I often put work above my relationship? (Yes/No)

What helps us find balance between responsibilities and love?

How can we honor God through both our work and our relationship?

## WEEKLY CHALLENGE

Set aside one "no work" evening this week to focus fully on each other.

Daily Prompts
Day 1: Read Colossians 3:23. How can I work for the Lord in my job?

Day 2: Journal one way work sometimes interferes with our time together.

Day 3: Write one boundary we could set for better balance.

Day 4: Pray and thank God for the blessing of work and provision.

Day 5: Share one joy from my work with my partner.

Day 6: Reflect: Did balancing work and love bring peace this week?

# Sabbath Rest Together

**WEEK 30**

**SCRIPTURE FOCUS**

"The Sabbath was made for man, not man for the Sabbath." — Mark 2:27

**DAY OF REST**

**SHORT LESSON:**

Rest is a gift from God, not just for the body but for the soul. Couples need time together in peace, away from stress, to focus on God and each other. Sabbath rest doesn't always mean a specific day, but it does mean intentional time set apart for worship, rest, and renewal. A relationship that embraces Sabbath learns to breathe, slow down, and be refreshed in God's presence.

**GUIDED PRAYER:**

Father,
Thank You for the gift of rest. Help us honor You by setting aside time to rest and worship. Teach us to slow down, recharge, and focus on what matters most.
Amen

**REFLECTION QUESTIONS:**

Do we intentionally make time for rest and worship together? (Yes/No)

What activities refresh us spiritually and emotionally?

How can Sabbath rest strengthen our relationship?

## WEEKLY CHALLENGE

Set aside one day or evening for rest, worship, and renewal together.

Daily Prompts
Day 1: Read Mark 2:27. Why did God design rest for us?

Day 2: Journal what makes me feel most rested.

Day 3: Write one way we can spend Sabbath time together this week.

Day 4: Pray together for peace and renewal.

Day 5: Share how rest changes my attitude and love toward my partner.

Day 6: Reflect: Did we experience God's peace in rest this week?

# Generosity & Giving

## WEEK 31

**SCRIPTURE FOCUS**

"Each of you should give what you have decided in your heart to give, not reluctantly or under compulsion, for God loves a cheerful giver." — 2 Corinthians 9:7

**SHORT LESSON:**

Generosity is love in action. God has given us everything—life, salvation, provision—and He calls us to live with open hands. Giving as a couple teaches trust, selflessness, and faith. When we give joyfully, we partner with God's work in the world and break free from selfishness. Generosity is not just about money; it includes time, encouragement, and kindness.

**GUIDED PRAYER:**

Lord,
Teach us to give with cheerful hearts. Help us to be generous with our time, our words, and our resources. May our giving reflect Your love and trust in Your provision.
Amen.

**REFLECTION QUESTIONS:**

Do we see generosity as a joy or a burden?

What is one way we can be more generous this week?

How does giving change the way we view money and time?

## WEEKLY CHALLENGE

Give something—money, time, or encouragement—together as a couple this week.

Daily Prompts
Day 1: Read 2 Corinthians 9:7 again. What does it mean to give "cheerfully," and what keeps me from doing that?

Day 2: Write about a time someone's generosity deeply impacted us. How did it make us feel?

Day 3: Identify one area where we could be more giving — money, time, encouragement, or forgiveness.

Day 4: Do a secret act of generosity for someone and write how it felt afterward.

Day 5: Pray for God to show us a person or need we can bless this week.

Day 6: Reflect: How did being generous together change our attitudes toward giving?

# Fasting & Seeking God

## WEEK 32

### SCRIPTURE FOCUS

"But when you fast, put oil on your head and wash your face, so that it will not be obvious to others that you are fasting, but only to your Father, who is unseen." — Matthew 6:17-18

### SHORT LESSON:

Fasting is about drawing closer to God by laying something aside to focus on Him. Couples who fast and pray together grow in discipline and faith. It could mean fasting from food, social media, or entertainment for a time. The goal is not to prove holiness but to seek God's presence more deeply. When a couple sets aside distractions and hungers for God, He meets them in powerful ways.

### GUIDED PRAYER:

Heavenly Father,
Teach us to fast with sincere hearts. Help us let go of distractions and turn to You with focus and hunger for Your presence. Draw us closer to You and to each other through this practice.
Amen.

### REFLECTION QUESTIONS:

Have we ever fasted together before? (Yes/No)

What could we give up temporarily to focus more on God?

How might fasting change our relationship with God?

## WEEKLY CHALLENGE

Choose one thing to fast from together this week and spend that time in prayer.

Daily Prompts:

Day 1: Read Matthew 6:17-18. What does fasting mean to you personally?

Day 2: Choose one thing to fast from this week. What will you focus on instead?

Day 3: Write a short prayer asking God to deepen your hunger for Him.

Day 4: How has fasting helped you hear God's voice more clearly?

Day 5: Journal one way fasting has changed your attitude or perspective.

Day 6: Reflect: What did God show you during this time of fasting and prayer?

# The Fruit of the Spirit in Marriage

## WEEK 33

Peace LOVE joy

### SCRIPTURE FOCUS

"But the fruit of the Spirit is love, joy, peace, forbearance, kindness, goodness, faithfulness, gentleness and self-control." — Galatians 5:22-23

### SHORT LESSON:

The Holy Spirit shapes us into the likeness of Christ by producing fruit in our lives. In relationships, these qualities bring joy, peace, and strength. Imagine a marriage filled with patience, kindness, and gentleness—it reflects God's kingdom. But fruit doesn't grow overnight; it takes time, prayer, and obedience. Couples who invite the Spirit to shape their hearts will see these qualities grow in their relationship.

### GUIDED PRAYER:

Holy Spirit,
Fill us with Your fruit. Grow love, joy, and peace in our relationship. Teach us patience, kindness, and self-control. May our relationship reflect the character of Christ.
Amen.

### REFLECTION QUESTIONS:

Which fruit of the Spirit do we see most in our relationship?

Which one do we need to grow in most right now?

How can we invite the Spirit to grow His fruit in us daily?

**WEEKLY CHALLENGE**

Choose one fruit of the Spirit to focus on together this week.

Daily Prompts:
Day 1: Read Galatians 5:22-23. Which fruit of the Spirit do we see most in our relationship?

Day 2: Write about one fruit we'd like to see grow more between us.

Day 3: What can we do differently this week to show love and kindness?

Day 4: Journal a moment this week when you felt peace or gentleness from your partner.

Day 5: Pray together for one specific fruit of the Spirit to grow.

Day 6: Reflect: How did walking in the Spirit change our relationship this week?

# Spiritual Warfare & Protection

## WEEK 34

### SCRIPTURE FOCUS

"Put on the full armor of God, so that you can take your stand against the devil's schemes." — Ephesians 6:11

### SHORT LESSON:

Relationships face not only daily struggles but spiritual battles. The enemy seeks to divide couples, discourage faith, and distract from God's purpose. God equips us with His armor—truth, righteousness, faith, prayer, and the Word. Couples who pray for protection and stand firm in Christ can overcome temptation and attack. Together, you are stronger when you stand in God's armor.

### GUIDED PRAYER:

Lord,
Protect us from the enemy's attacks. Clothe us in Your armor and remind us that we fight not against each other, but against spiritual forces. Keep us united and strong in Your truth.
Amen.

### REFLECTION QUESTIONS:

Do we pray for protection over our relationship regularly? (Yes/No)

What spiritual distractions or temptations do we need to guard against?

How does remembering we are on the same team change conflict?

## WEEKLY CHALLENGE

Pray Ephesians 6:10-18 together daily this week.

Daily Prompts:

Day 1: Read Ephesians 6:10-11. What piece of the armor of God do we need most right now?

Day 2: Write a short prayer asking God to protect your relationship.

Day 3: Identify one area where the enemy tries to cause division and pray over it

Day 4: Journal how God has shown protection in your life recently.

Day 5: Memorize one verse from Ephesians 6 together. Write it down here.

Day 6: Reflect: How did prayer and awareness strengthen our unity this week?

# Overcoming Temptation Together

## WEEK 35

### SCRIPTURE FOCUS

### SHORT LESSON:

Temptation is a reality for everyone, but God always provides a way out. Couples must be honest about struggles and support each other in choosing holiness. Whether it's lust, anger, selfishness, or distraction, overcoming temptation requires prayer, accountability, and God's strength. Victory comes not from willpower but from dependence on Christ.

### GUIDED PRAYER:

Dear Lord Jesus,

You walked this earth and faced temptation just as we do. Yet You overcame by the power of the Word. When the enemy came, You declared with authority, "It is written." Your truth silenced every lie. Teach us to do the same, Lord —to meet every temptation with what is written in Your Word.
Give us strength to choose what is right, and courage to support one another in holiness.
Let Your Word be alive within us — a sword of truth, a shield of faith, our defense when we are weak, our victory when we stand firm in You. For it is written: "Greater is He that is in you than he that is in the world." And we stand on that promise today.

Amen

### REFLECTION QUESTIONS:

What temptations do we face most as a couple?

How can we hold each other accountable in love?

How has God helped me overcome temptation in the past?

## WEEKLY CHALLENGE

Talk openly about one area of temptation and pray over it daily this week.

Daily Prompts:
Day 1: Read 1 Corinthians 10:13. What does this verse teach us about God's faithfulness?

Day 2: Identify one temptation we need to be honest about with each other.

Day 3: Pray for strength and accountability in that area.

Day 4: Write one practical step to avoid temptation this week.

Day 5: Encourage each other with one Bible verse about victory in Christ.

Day 6: Reflect: How did honesty and prayer bring freedom this week?

Reflection: Overcoming Modern-Day Temptations

Temptation doesn't always come in obvious forms. It can appear in small daily choices — in words, habits, and thoughts.

Jesus faced temptation too, but He overcame by standing on God's Word, saying, "It is written." That same Word is our defense today. God promises that when we are tempted, He will always provide a way out.

## 🌿 Common Modern-Day Temptations

<u>Comparison</u> → Scrolling through social media and feeling "less than" or resentful. Temptation: to envy others or doubt God's plan. Truth: "Be content with what you have." — Hebrews 13:5

<u>Compromise</u> → Ignoring biblical convictions to fit in or avoid conflict. Temptation: to please people instead of pleasing God. Truth: "We must obey God rather than men." — Acts 5:29

<u>Lust & Impurity</u> → Entertaining inappropriate thoughts, images, or entertainment. Temptation: to treat desire lightly. Truth: "Blessed are the pure in heart, for they shall see God." — Matthew 5:8

<u>Pride</u> → Needing to be right, prove a point, or get the last word. Temptation: to put self above others.
Truth: "God opposes the proud but gives grace to the humble." — James 4:6

<u>Neglecting God</u> → Filling every moment with noise or busyness, leaving no time for prayer or Scripture. Temptation: to rely on self instead of the Spirit. Truth: "Be still and know that I am God." — Psalm 46:10

<u>Bitterness & Unforgiveness</u> → Holding onto hurt or anger instead of releasing it. Temptation: to let resentment harden your heart. Truth: "Forgive as the Lord forgave you." — Colossians 3:13

## 🌿 Reflection Prompts

Which of these temptations do we face most often as a couple?

What truth from God's Word can help us resist when it comes again?

How can we remind each other to respond like Jesus—with "It is written" instead of reacting in weakness?

## 🌿 Practical Steps

Keep a verse handy to speak when temptation strikes.

Replace tempting habits with prayer, worship, or a walk outside.

Be honest with your partner—confession breaks the power of secrecy.

Celebrate small victories together.

## 🌿 A Closing Prayer

Lord Jesus,

You conquered temptation with the Word of God. Help us remember that same power lives within us. Give us strength to resist, courage to confess, and faith to stand firm. Let what is written be our guide and our defense.

Amen.

More in Depth with Proverbs 14:12
"There is a way that seems right to a man, but its end is the way to death."

A Note About "Death" and God's Justice

At first, the word death in this verse can feel unsettling — even frightening. Many of us are more comfortable thinking of God only as loving, gentle, and forgiving (and He truly is all of those things).  But God's love is complete, and complete love also includes justice, truth, and correction. When Scripture speaks of "death" here, it doesn't only mean physical death. It points to spiritual separation from God — the distance that forms when we choose our own way instead of His.
 Like a loving parent warning a child not to run into traffic, God warns us because He wants to protect us, not punish us. His justice is real and it's the proof of His deep care for our souls. For couples, this verse is a loving reminder:  When you walk away from God's wisdom, you walk toward emptiness — but when you walk with Him, you walk toward life, peace, and unity.

Here's a clear, layered explanation of what Proverbs 14:12 means:

The Surface Meaning

At first glance, this verse warns that human judgment is limited and often deceiving. People can convince themselves that their choices, attitudes, or lifestyles are right— even morally or spiritually acceptable—when in truth, those choices lead to destruction. The "way" represents a chosen path, habit, or way of living that feels right emotionally or logically but isn't aligned with God's truth.

The Spiritual Lesson

The verse highlights the danger of self-reliance without divine guidance. It's easy to mistake personal reasoning, cultural approval, or emotions for what's "right." However, what feels right is not always what is right in God's eyes. Scripture consistently reminds us that human wisdom apart from God leads to spiritual death.
(see Proverbs 3:5-6: "Trust in the Lord with all your heart and lean not on your own understanding").

continued reflection on page 93

# Gratitude & Thanksgiving

## WEEK 36

### SCRIPTURE FOCUS

"Give thanks in all circumstances; for this is God's will for you in Christ Jesus." — 1 Thessalonians 5:18

### SHORT LESSON:

Gratitude transforms relationships. Choosing thankfulness shifts focus from problems to blessings. When couples practice thanksgiving, even in challenges, joy grows and love deepens. Gratitude is not ignoring struggles but choosing to see God's goodness in every circumstance. A thankful heart builds resilience, hope, and encouragement in your relationship.

### GUIDED PRAYER:

Dear Lord,
Thank You for your endless grace and mercies. Thank You for every blessing You've given us. Help us to live with thankful hearts, seeing Your goodness in every situation. Teach us to encourage each other with gratitude daily.
Amen.

### REFLECTION QUESTIONS:

Do I express gratitude to God and my partner often enough?

What blessings can we thank God for this week?

## WEEKLY CHALLENGE

Each day this week, thank God for one blessing and tell your partner one thing you appreciate about them.

Daily Prompts:

Day 1: Write down three blessings from this week.
1.

2.

3.

Day 2: Thank God out loud for one thing about your partner.

Day 3: Read 1 Thessalonians 5:18. How can we give thanks in every circumstance?

Day 4: Journal a moment when gratitude replaced frustration.

Day 5: Write a short note of thanks to your partner or someone else. Give it to them.

Day 6: Reflect: How did practicing gratitude change our attitude this week?

# *Persevering Through Trials*

## WEEK 37

### SCRIPTURE FOCUS

"Consider it pure joy, my brothers and sisters, whenever you face trials of many kinds, because you know that the testing of your faith produces perseverance." — James 1:2-3

### SHORT LESSON:

Every couple faces trials—financial struggles, health issues, disagreements, or disappointments. Trials test faith but also produce perseverance and maturity. Instead of running from challenges, God calls couples to trust Him and endure with hope. When you face trials together, leaning on God and each other, your love becomes stronger and deeper.

### GUIDED PRAYER:

Lord,
Strengthen us in trials. Help us see challenges not as setbacks but as opportunities to grow in faith and love. Give us patience and perseverance to endure together with hope.
Amen.

### REFLECTION QUESTIONS:

What trial are we currently facing, and how can we trust God with it?

How have past trials strengthened our relationship?

How does perseverance reflect faith in God?

## WEEKLY CHALLENGE

Choose one current struggle and pray for endurance over it daily this week.

Daily Prompts:

Day 1: Read James 1:2-3. What trial are we facing right now?

Day 2: Write about a time God strengthened us in hardship.

Day 3: Pray together for endurance and unity.

Day 4: Journal one lesson God might be teaching us through this trial.

Day 5: Encourage each other with a verse about hope.

Day 6: Reflect: How did this week grow our faith as a couple?

## Persevering Through Trials

Trials are not meant to destroy us — they are meant to develop us. When life feels heavy, when prayers seem unanswered, and when faith is tested, God is not absent. He is refining us. Perseverance is built in the waiting, the enduring, and the trusting.   As a couple, facing trials together can either divide or strengthen you — the difference lies in whether you face them with God or without Him.

### 🌿 God's Word on Perseverance

Trials Strengthen Faith: "Consider it pure joy, my brothers and sisters, whenever you face trials of many kinds, because you know that the testing of your faith produces perseverance." — James 1:2-3. Every hardship has a purpose. God uses pain to produce endurance and maturity.
God Is with You in the Fire "When you pass through the waters, I will be with you; and when you walk through the fire, you will not be burned." — Isaiah 43:2. You are not alone in difficulty. God's presence is your protection.
Hope Anchors the Soul: "We have this hope as an anchor for the soul, firm and secure." — Hebrews 6:19. Hope in Christ keeps you steady when storms come.

### 🌿 Real-Life Examples of Modern Trials

Financial Pressure → Trusting God when bills are due or when income is uncertain.
Lesson: Trials teach us to rely on God's provision, not our plans.

Health Issues  → Walking through sickness or chronic pain.
Lesson: Faith deepens when we choose gratitude and peace despite the struggle.

Relationship Conflicts →Misunderstandings, hurt feelings, or distance in communication.
Lesson: Perseverance means loving even when it's hard and forgiving quickly.

Spiritual Dryness → Feeling distant from God or questioning His plan.
Lesson: Keep showing up. Faith grows most when feelings fade.

Waiting Seasons → Waiting for direction, healing, or breakthrough.
Lesson: God often works in silence; waiting is a form of worship.

### 🌿 Practical Steps to Persevere Together

Pray together even when you don't feel like it.
Speak faith instead of fear — remind each other of what God has already done.
Keep a "Victory Journal" — record answered prayers and breakthroughs, big or small.
Encourage each other daily with one Scripture or affirmation of hope.
Worship together — praise is often the key that breaks discouragement.

### 🌿 A Couple's Prayer

Dear Lord, Trials are difficult. In our trials, teach us endurance. When we grow weary, remind us that You are working all things for our good.  Help us stand firm, love deeply, and trust fully. Make our relationship stronger through every storm. May our perseverance reflect our faith in You. Amen.

Continued from page 87

Proverbs 14:12
"There is a way that seems right to a man, but its end is the way to death."

Isaiah 59:2
"But your iniquities have made a separation between you and your God, and your sins have hidden His face from you so that He does not hear."

### The Deeper Connection to Isaiah 59:2

Isaiah 59:2 reinforces this idea by showing the consequence of living by our own way: sin separates us from God. When we follow what "seems right" instead of what is right according to God's word, we end up walking away from His presence and protection. The "death" mentioned in Proverbs isn't only physical—it can mean spiritual emptiness, separation from God, or even eternal loss.

### The Application

This proverb invites us to:
- Pause before acting on instinct or emotion and instead ask God for discernment.
- Compare our choices to Scripture rather than to what society or others say is acceptable.
- Pray for alignment between our thoughts and God's truth, remembering that His ways lead to life and peace.

Proverbs 14:12 is a sober reminder that human reasoning without God's guidance is a dangerous path. God's character and truth are unchanging. We are not meant to redefine Him or reinterpret Scripture to make our way of living feel right. When we try to mold God to fit our perception of what's acceptable, we create an idol — a version of God that serves us, rather than us serving Him.
The call of faith is to conform our lives to God's Word, not to conform His Word to our lives. True safety and life come from walking in God's wisdom, not our own understanding.

continued reflection on page 99

# Handling Fear & Anxiety

## WEEK 38

### SCRIPTURE FOCUS

"Cast all your anxiety on him because he cares for you." –
1 Peter 5:7

### SHORT LESSON:

Fear and anxiety can weigh heavily on couples. Worry about the future, finances, or health can create tension. But God calls us to cast our cares on Him because He loves us deeply. Releasing anxiety to God frees couples from carrying burdens alone. Together, you can replace worry with prayer, fear with trust, and anxiety with peace.

### GUIDED PRAYER:

Father,
We give You our fears and anxieties. Remind us that You care for us and hold our future. Replace our worry with peace and our fear with trust in You.
Amen.

### REFLECTION QUESTIONS:

What do we worry about most as a couple?

How can we remind each other to cast our cares on God?

What Scripture brings me peace when I feel anxious?

## WEEKLY CHALLENGE

Whenever anxiety arises this week, stop and pray together immediately.

Daily Prompts:

Day 1: Read James 1:2-3. What trial are we facing right now?

Day 2: Write about a time God strengthened us in hardship.

Day 3: Pray together for endurance and unity.

Day 4: Journal one lesson God might be teaching us through this trial.

Day 5: Encourage each other with a verse about hope.

Day 6: Reflect: How did this week grow our faith as a couple?

# Speaking Life Over Each Other

## WEEK 39

### SCRIPTURE FOCUS

"The tongue has the power of life and death, and those who love it will eat its fruit." — Proverbs 18:21

### SHORT LESSON:

Words carry power. They can build up or tear down, encourage or discourage. Speaking life means choosing words of hope, blessing, and love, even in hard times. Couples who practice speaking life strengthen trust, joy, and intimacy. God calls us to let our words be filled with grace and truth, bringing healing instead of harm.

### GUIDED PRAYER:

Lord,
Help us to speak life over each other daily. Forgive us for words that have hurt. Teach us to use our tongues to bless, encourage, and honor one another.
Amen.

### REFLECTION QUESTIONS:

What do I think my words more often do: build up or tear down? (Have your partner answer this question about how they feel about your words.)

What words of life mean the most to me?

How can I speak blessing over my partner this week?

## WEEKLY CHALLENGE

Speak one word of life and encouragement to your partner each day this week

Daily Prompts
Day 1: Read Proverbs 18:21. What words do I speak most often—life or frustration?


Day 2: Speak one word of blessing over your partner and write how they responded.


Day 3: Pray and ask God to help you guard your tongue this week.

Day 4: Journal a time this week when your partner's words lifted your spirit


Day 5: Write one truth from Scripture to speak over each other daily.


Day 6: Reflect: How did our words affect our connection this week?

## Speaking Life Over Each Other

Words carry power — the power to build up or tear down, to heal or to wound. As a couple, the way you speak to and about each other sets the atmosphere of your home. When you choose to speak life — words of encouragement, truth, and blessing — you invite God's presence into your relationship. When you speak carelessly, you create space for division, discouragement, and doubt. Speaking life isn't pretending everything is perfect; it's choosing to see your partner as God sees them — loved, valuable, and in progress.

### ✤ God's Word on the Power of Words

Words Have Consequences: "The tongue has the power of life and death, and those who love it will eat its fruit." — Proverbs 18:21 → Every word you speak either nourishes or poisons your relationship.
Speak with Grace: "Let your conversation be always full of grace, seasoned with salt, so that you may know how to answer everyone." — Colossians 4:6 → Grace-filled words reflect Christ and bring peace.
Encouragement Builds Strength "Therefore encourage one another and build each other up." — 1 Thessalonians 5:11 → Your partner needs your encouragement more than your criticism.

### ✤ Examples of Speaking Life

Blessing Instead of Criticism
  → Instead of, "You never help enough." say, "I really appreciate when you help — it means a lot to me."
Encouragement Instead of Complaint
  → "You handled that situation with such patience. I admire that."
Gratitude Instead of Neglect
  → "Thank you for working so hard for our family."
Prayer Instead of Gossip
  → When you're frustrated, pray for your partner instead of venting to others.
Affirmation Instead of Comparison
  → "You are exactly who God made you to be, and I'm thankful for that."

### ✤ Reflection Prompts

What kind of words do we speak most often — life-giving or draining?
How can we create a habit of encouraging each other daily?
What phrase or truth from Scripture could we speak over one another this week?

### ✤ Practical Ways to Speak Life

Start each day with one word of blessing or appreciation.
When conflict arises, pause and pray before responding.
Keep a shared "Words of Life" page — write kind things you notice about each other.
End each day by saying one thing you're grateful for in your partner.
Replace "You always…" and "You never…" with "I feel…" or "I appreciate when…"

### ✤ A Couple's Prayer

Lord, Let our words bring life, not harm. Teach us to speak with kindness, grace, and truth.
 Help us see each other through Your eyes and use our voices to bless, not to break.
 May every word we speak draw us closer to You and to each other.   Amen.

continued from page 99

## Truth Spotlight: Don't Reshape God to Fit Your Way

Remember:
- We can't mold God to fit our lifestyle or justify our choices.
- His truth doesn't shift to match what feels comfortable or acceptable to us.
- When we reshape God to fit our perception of what's "okay," we create a version of Him that serves us—rather than letting our lives serve Him.
- Real faith means letting God's Word shape our hearts and habits, even when it challenges what we want.

Romans 12:2
"Do not be conformed to this world, but be transformed by the renewal of your mind."

Isaiah 55:8-9
"For my thoughts are not your thoughts, neither are your ways my ways," declares the Lord. "For as the heavens are higher than the earth, so are my ways higher than your ways and my thoughts than your thoughts.

Reflection Questions
- Are there areas in our relationship where we've been doing what feels right instead of seeking God's direction? Discuss with your partner or write in a journal.
- How can we remind each other to check our choices against God's Word before making decisions?
- What does surrendering to God's truth look like in our daily lives together?

continued on page 107

# Growing in Hope & Purpose

## WEEK 40

### SCRIPTURE FOCUS

"For I know the plans I have for you," declares the Lord, "plans to prosper you and not to harm you, plans to give you hope and a future." — Jeremiah 29:11

### SHORT LESSON:

Hope anchors relationships in God's promises. When couples focus on God's purpose for their future, they live with joy and expectation. Hope doesn't mean everything will be easy, but it does mean everything is in God's hands. A couple who places their hope in God finds strength in trials, joy in waiting, and purpose in every season of life.

### GUIDED PRAYER:

Father,
Thank You for giving us hope and purpose. Help us to trust Your plans for our future. Keep our hearts focused on Your promises and strengthen our faith in every season.
Amen.

### REFLECTION QUESTIONS:

Where do we place our hope most often—God or circumstances?

What purpose do we believe God has for us as a couple?

How does hope in God change the way we face challenges?

## WEEKLY CHALLENGE

Write down a shared vision for your future as a couple and pray over it this week.

Daily Prompts
Day 1: Read Jeremiah 29:11. What promise stands out to you most?

Day 2: Write one dream or goal you're trusting God with right now.

Day 3: Pray together about your shared future.

Day 4: Journal one way God has already shown His purpose in your relationship.

Day 5: Write a verse or affirmation about hope to remind yourself daily.

Day 6: Reflect: How did hope shape our outlook this week?

# Raising Children in Faith

## WEEK 41

### SCRIPTURE FOCUS

"Fathers, do not exasperate your children; instead, bring them up in the training and instruction of the Lord." — Ephesians 6:4

### SHORT LESSON:

Children are a blessing and responsibility from the Lord. Whether you are parents now or preparing for the future, your role is to teach them the ways of God. Faith is caught as much as taught—children learn by watching how you live. A couple that prays, worships, and obeys God models faith that lasts generations.

### GUIDED PRAYER:

Father,
Thank You for the gift of children, present or future. Help us lead by example, teaching faith with patience, love, and truth. Let our home be a place where Your Word is honored.
Amen.

### REFLECTION QUESTIONS:

What faith practices do I want to model for my children (neices, nephews, other's children?)

How can we pray for our children daily (born or unborn)?

Why is it important to disciple children at home, not just at church?

## WEEKLY CHALLENGE

Pray together daily for your children—or for the future children God may give.

Daily Prompts:
Day 1: Read Ephesians 6:4. What does it mean to "bring them up in the Lord"?

Day 2: Pray for wisdom to guide future or current children.

Day 3: Journal one faith habit you want to model for them.

Day 4: Write a short prayer of blessing for your children (or future children).

Day 5: Discuss one family value you want to pass down.

Day 6: Reflect: How does thinking about legacy change how we live now?

# Leaving a Legacy of Faith

**SCRIPTURE FOCUS**

"But from everlasting to everlasting the Lord's love is with those who fear him, and his righteousness with their children's children." — Psalm 103:17

**SHORT LESSON:**

A true legacy is not wealth or possessions but faith passed to the next generation. Couples have the privilege to influence not only their children but their grandchildren and beyond. Living faithfully today impacts tomorrow. What you sow now—prayer, love, integrity—becomes seeds for future generations to reap.

**GUIDED PRAYER:**

Lord,
Help us leave a legacy of faith. Teach us to live in ways that honor You and inspire the generations after us to trust You. May our love for You echo in our family for years to come.
Amen.

**REFLECTION QUESTIONS:**

What kind of spiritual legacy do I want to leave behind?

How can we live today to bless tomorrow's generations?

What godly influences from the past inspire me?

## WEEKLY CHALLENGE

Write a prayer or blessing for future generations of your family.

Daily Prompts:

Day 1: Read Psalm 103:17. What kind of legacy do we want to leave?

Day 2: Write down one example of faith from a parent or mentor who inspires you.

Day 3: Pray for future generations of your family to know Christ.

Day 4: Journal a way to share your faith story with others.

Day 5: Write one tradition you can start that keeps God at the cente

Day 6: Reflect: How does leaving a legacy motivate us to live faithfully today?

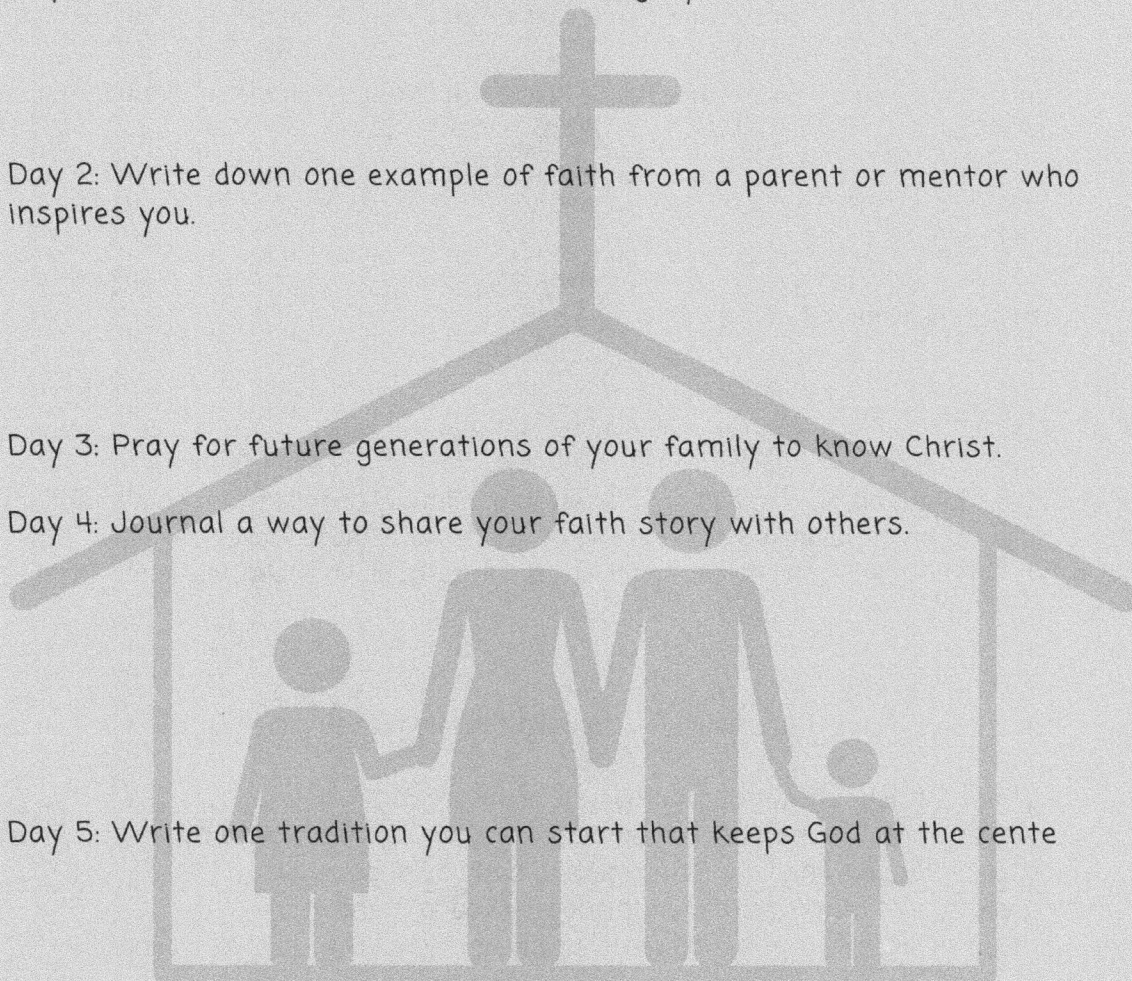

## Leaving a Legacy of Faith

A legacy isn't about what we own — it's about what we pass on. The love, faith, and wisdom you live out today can echo through generations tomorrow. Every choice, every prayer, every act of kindness leaves fingerprints of God's grace for others to follow. You don't have to be perfect to leave a godly legacy — you just have to be faithful. When you love like Jesus, forgive quickly, and keep pointing people toward Him, you plant seeds that outlive you.

### ✤ God's Word on Legacy

"But from everlasting to everlasting the Lord's love is with those who fear Him, and His righteousness with their children's children." — Psalm 103:17

"Train up a child in the way he should go, and when he is old he will not depart from it." — Proverbs 22:6
"Let your light shine before others, that they may see your good deeds and glorify your Father in heaven." — Matthew 5:16

### ✤ Reflection Prompts

What kind of faith do we want to pass down to our family or those who know us?
What daily habits or values reflect the kind of legacy we want to leave?
Who has left a lasting spiritual impact on our lives, and what can we learn from their example?

### ✤ Practical Ways to Build a Godly Legacy

Pray together for your children, grandchildren, or future family.
Keep a prayer journal that others can someday read and be encouraged by.
Live transparently, showing how faith works in both joy and hardship.
Serve together — let others see Christ in the way you love and give. 106
Speak blessings often — your words can shape hearts long after they're spoken.

### ✤ A Couple's Prayer
Lord,
Thank You for the gift of faith and the privilege of passing it on. Help us live in a way that reflects Your love and truth. Let our home be a light that points others to You. May the legacy we leave be one of faith, forgiveness, and steadfast love. Amen.

continued from page   99

## Quiet Reflection

Before you answer the reflection questions below, take a moment to pray together. Ask God to open your hearts to His truth and reveal any areas of your life or relationship where you've been relying on what "feels right" instead of what is right in His Word.

## 💬 Reflection Questions

1. Have we ever justified something because it felt right at the time, but later realized it wasn't aligned with God's will?
   - Example Response: "We used to make quick decisions without praying first. We both saw later how those choices caused unnecessary stress."
2. In what areas of our relationship might we be shaping God's truth to fit our comfort?
   - Example Response: "We sometimes avoid hard conversations about faith or boundaries because it's easier to keep peace than to face conviction."
3. What helps us recognize the Holy Spirit's guidance — that inner peace or unease — when making decisions?
   - Example Response: "When we both sense peace about a choice after prayer, we know God's confirming it. If one of us feels unsettled, we've learned to wait."
4. How can we remind each other to pause and pray before major decisions?
   - Example Response: "We could start praying together on Sunday evenings for our week ahead — that would help us stay aligned."
5. What does it mean for our relationship to be shaped by God's truth rather than our own desires?
   - Example Response: "It means letting the Bible, not emotions, guide our words and actions — especially when we disagree."

## 🖋 Prayer Space

"Lord, help us walk in Your truth even when it challenges our comfort. Holy Spirit, align our thoughts with godly thoughts.  Keep us sensitive to Your Spirit, humble in correction, and united in purpose. Teach us to love Your ways more than our own. Amen."

# Evangelism as a Couple

## SCRIPTURE FOCUS

> "Therefore go and make disciples of all nations, baptizing them in the name of the Father and of the Son and of the Holy Spirit." — Matthew 28:19

## SHORT LESSON:

The Great Commission is not just for individuals but for couples too. Together, you can share the love of Christ with neighbors, co-workers, friends, and family. Evangelism may look like inviting someone to church, praying for a friend, or living with integrity. When couples witness together, they reflect God's love in powerful ways.

## GUIDED PRAYER:

Jesus,
Give us boldness to share Your love as a couple. Show us opportunities to witness and give us wisdom to speak with grace and truth. Use our relationship to draw others to You.
Amen.

## REFLECTION QUESTIONS:

Do people see Christ in the way we live and love?

Who can we pray for together this week to come to know Jesus?

How does serving God together strengthen our relationship?

## WEEKLY CHALLENGE

Share your faith as a couple with one person this week.

Daily Prompts:
Day 1: Read Matthew 28:19-20. Who could we pray for this week to know Jesus?

Day 2: Write one way we can show Christ's love to others through action.

Day 3: Pray for boldness to share your testimony.

Day 4: Journal a conversation where you sensed God prompting you to speak.

Day 5: Thank God for using your relationship as a light to others.

Day 6: Reflect: How did sharing our faith strengthen our unity this week?

# Serving in the Church

## WEEK 44

### SCRIPTURE FOCUS

"Now you are the body of Christ, and each one of you is a part of it." —
1 Corinthians 12:27

### SHORT LESSON:

God designed the church as a body, with each member serving a role. Couples who serve together strengthen both their church and their relationship. Serving can mean teaching, helping, encouraging, or supporting in practical ways. When you serve in unity, you grow closer to each other and to God's people.

### GUIDED PRAYER:

Lord,
Thank You for placing us in Your body, the church. Show us where we can serve together. Use our gifts to bless others and build up Your people.
In Jesus' Holy Name, Amen

### REFLECTION QUESTIONS:

Are we members of a church? Yes/No.

Where are we currently serving in the church?

What gifts has God given us that we could use to serve?

How does serving together bring us closer?

## WEEKLY CHALLENGE

Choose one area in your church where you can serve side by side.

Daily Prompts:

Day 1: Read 1 Corinthians 12:27. What role do we feel called to play in the church?

Day 2: Journal one area of need we could help meet this month.

Day 3: Pray for your pastors and church leaders.

Day 4: Volunteer or encourage someone serving faithfully.

Day 5: Write how serving together made you feel closer to God.

Day 6: Reflect: How does serving in the body of Christ grow our relationship?

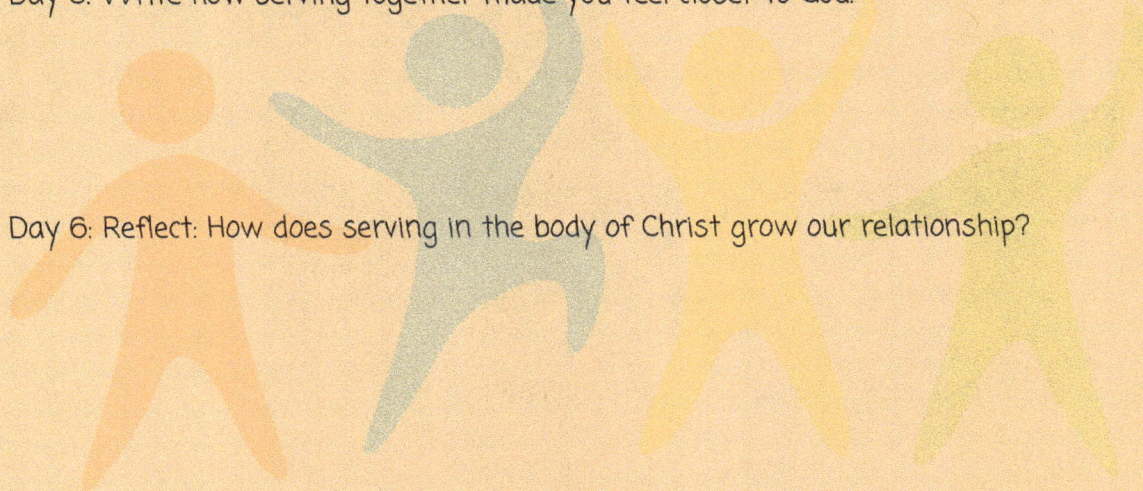

# Enduring Faith

## WEEK 45

### SCRIPTURE FOCUS

"Let us run with perseverance the race marked out for us, fixing our eyes on Jesus." — Hebrews 12:1-2

### SHORT LESSON:

Faith is a marathon, not a sprint. Couples must endure seasons of joy and hardship with steady perseverance. The key is keeping eyes fixed on Jesus. When struggles come, remember the goal—eternal life with Christ. Enduring together makes love stronger and faith deeper.

### GUIDED PRAYER:

Lord,
Strengthen our faith to endure. Help us fix our eyes on Jesus and run the race with perseverance. Keep us faithful through every season.
Amen.

### REFLECTION QUESTIONS:

When have we wanted to give up, and how did God sustain us?

How can we encourage each other to stay faithful long-term?

What habits keep our eyes fixed on Jesus?

## WEEKLY CHALLENGE

Encourage each other daily with one word of faith and hope.

Daily Prompts:

Day 1: Read Hebrews 12:1-2. What helps you keep your eyes on Jesus?

Day 2: Write a prayer for endurance in faith.

Day 3: Encourage your partner with a verse about perseverance.

Day 4: Journal a time when faith carried you through hardship.

Day 5: Pray for the strength to stay faithful in future seasons.

Day 6: Reflect: How did perseverance deepen our love for God and each other?

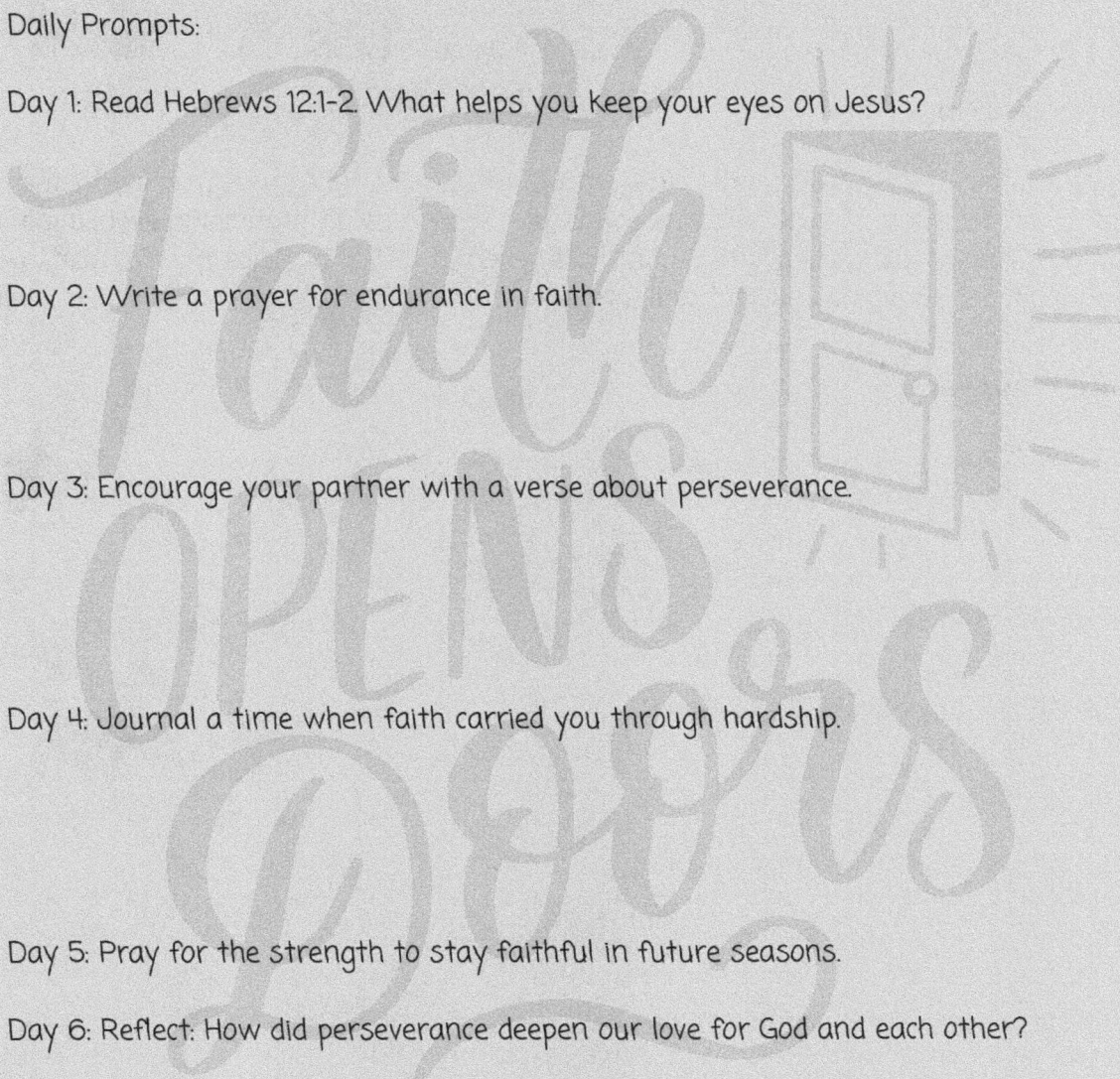

# Joy in All Circumstances

## WEEK 46

**Seek Joy**

### SCRIPTURE FOCUS

"Rejoice in the Lord always. I will say it again: Rejoice!" — Philippians 4:4

### SHORT LESSON:

Joy is not based on circumstances but on Christ. Couples who root their joy in the Lord find strength no matter what happens. Joy doesn't mean pretending everything is fine—it means choosing gratitude and faith even in difficulty. Rejoicing together in God's goodness keeps hearts light and love alive.

### GUIDED PRAYER:

Lord,
Teach us to rejoice in You always. Fill our hearts with joy that comes from Your Spirit, not from circumstances. May our relationship radiate hope and gladness.
Amen.

### REFLECTION QUESTIONS:

Do I often confuse joy with happiness?

How can we rejoice together in hard times?

What blessings bring us joy in this season?

## WEEKLY CHALLENGE

Each day this week, write down one reason to rejoice in God.

Daily Prompts:
Day 1: Read Philippians 4:4. What does it mean to "rejoice always"?

Day 2: Write down three small joys from today.

Day 3: Pray for joy to replace stress or discouragement.

Day 4: Journal a moment when laughter or joy brought peace this week.

Day 5: Share something that makes you both smile and thank God for it.

Day 6: Reflect: How did choosing joy affect our attitudes this week?

# Living by Faith, Not by Sight

## WEEK 47

### SCRIPTURE FOCUS

"For we live by faith, not by sight." — 2 Corinthians 5:7
Now faith is the substance of things hoped for, the evidence of things not seen."
— Hebrews 11:1.

### SHORT LESSON:

Faith means trusting God even when the path ahead is unclear. Couples who live by faith lean on God's promises, not on what they see or feel. Fear fades when faith grows. Walking by faith as a couple means surrendering plans, trusting God's timing, and stepping forward with confidence in Him

### GUIDED PRAYER:

Dear Heavenly Father,
Your Word tells us that faith is confidence in what we hope for and assurance in what we do not see. Teach us to walk in that kind of faith — to trust Your promises even when the path is unclear. Help us study Your Word so we can recognize Your voice and follow Your direction. Strengthen our hearts to rely fully on You — our unchanging, faithful, and good God. May our faith not rest on what we see, but on who You are.
Amen.

### REFLECTION QUESTIONS:

What situation in our lives requires more faith right now?


Do I trust God's promises more than my own plans?


How does faith shape the way we love each other?

## WEEKLY CHALLENGE

- Take one step of faith together this week in an area you've been hesitant. Examples: l
- Spiritual Growth → "We've talked about joining a church small group for months — this week we'll finally sign up."
- Financial Trust → "We've been afraid to tithe or give regularly, but this week we'll trust God by giving first."
- Forgiveness → "We'll reach out to a family member we've been avoiding and choose to forgive."
- Service → "We'll volunteer together at church or in the community, even if it feels uncomfortable at first."
- Future Decisions → "We'll pray and take one practical step toward a big decision we've been putting off — like applying for a new job, moving forward with counseling, or planning a wedding rooted in faith."
- Public Faith → "We'll pray together in public before eating, even if it feels awkward."

Daily Prompts:

Day 1: Read 2 Corinthians 5:7. What area requires faith right now? "Now faith is the substance of things hoped for, the evidence of things not seen. "Hebrews 11:1. It describes faith as a confident assurance or firm conviction of what is hoped for and a demonstrated reality of things that are unseen.

Day 2: Write a prayer of trust for what you cannot yet see.

Day 3: Journal one time God proved faithful in the past.

Day 4: Encourage each other with a reminder of God's promises.

Day 5: Pray and thank God for His guidance, even when the path is unclear.

Day 6: Reflect: How did walking by faith bring peace this week?

# The Power of Prayer & Fasting Together

**THE POWER OF PRAYER**

## WEEK 48

### SCRIPTURE FOCUS

This kind can come out only by prayer and fasting." — Mark 9:29

### SHORT LESSON:

Mark 9:29: The verse teaches that true ministry requires a deep, constant reliance on God, rather than on any inherent ability or authority the disciples may have. Prayer and fasting together unleash spiritual power. Some battles require deeper surrender and focus. Couples who unite in prayer and fasting grow closer to God and see breakthroughs. Whether praying for healing, provision, or direction, fasting intensifies prayer by putting God above all else.

### GUIDED PRAYER:

Oh Gracious and Mighty Lord,
Teach us the power of prayer and fasting. Unite our hearts as
we seek You with focus and faith. Bring breakthroughs in our
lives as we surrender fully.
We give you all the glory, God. Amen.

### REFLECTION QUESTIONS:

Do we truly believe in the power of prayer and fasting? yes/no

What breakthrough are we seeking from God?

How can we encourage each other during times of fasting?

## WEEKLY CHALLENGE

Dedicate one day this week to pray and fast together.

Daily Prompts:
Day 1: Read Mark 9:29. Why do you think prayer and fasting are powerful together?

Day 2: Choose a shared prayer focus for this week.

Day 3: Write how fasting deepens your dependence on God.

Day 4: Journal what you sense God speaking during prayer time.

Day 5: Prayer to thank God for any peace or breakthrough you've seen.

Day 6: Reflect: What did God reveal through our prayer and fasting?

# *Preparing for Eternity Together*

## WEEK 49

### SCRIPTURE FOCUS

> "But our citizenship is in heaven. And we eagerly await a Savior from there, the Lord Jesus Christ." — Philippians 3:20

### SHORT LESSON:

This world is temporary, but eternity with Christ is forever. Couples who live with eternity in mind keep perspective during trials. Preparing for eternity means fixing your eyes on Jesus, living with hope, and helping each other stay faithful. True love points to eternal love with Christ.

### GUIDED PRAYER:

Jesus,
You said in your word in John 14:2, "'In my Father's house are many mansions; if it were not so, I would have told you. I go to prepare a place for you." Thank You for preparing a place for us. Help us live with eternity in mind and encourage each other to stay faithful until the end. May our love point to You always.
Amen.

### REFLECTION QUESTIONS:

Do we think about eternity often, or just the present?

How can remembering heaven change our daily choices?

How do we encourage each other to live with eternity in view?

## WEEKLY CHALLENGE

Talk about what eternity with Christ means to each of you.

Daily Prompts:

Day 1: Read Philippians 3:20. What does it mean to live as citizens of heaven?

Day 2: Journal one way to live with eternity in mind this week.

Day 3: Pray for strength to live faithfully today.

Day 4: Write about something you look forward to in eternity.

Day 5: Encourage each other to stay focused on eternal things.

Day 6: Reflect: How did remembering heaven change our priorities this week?

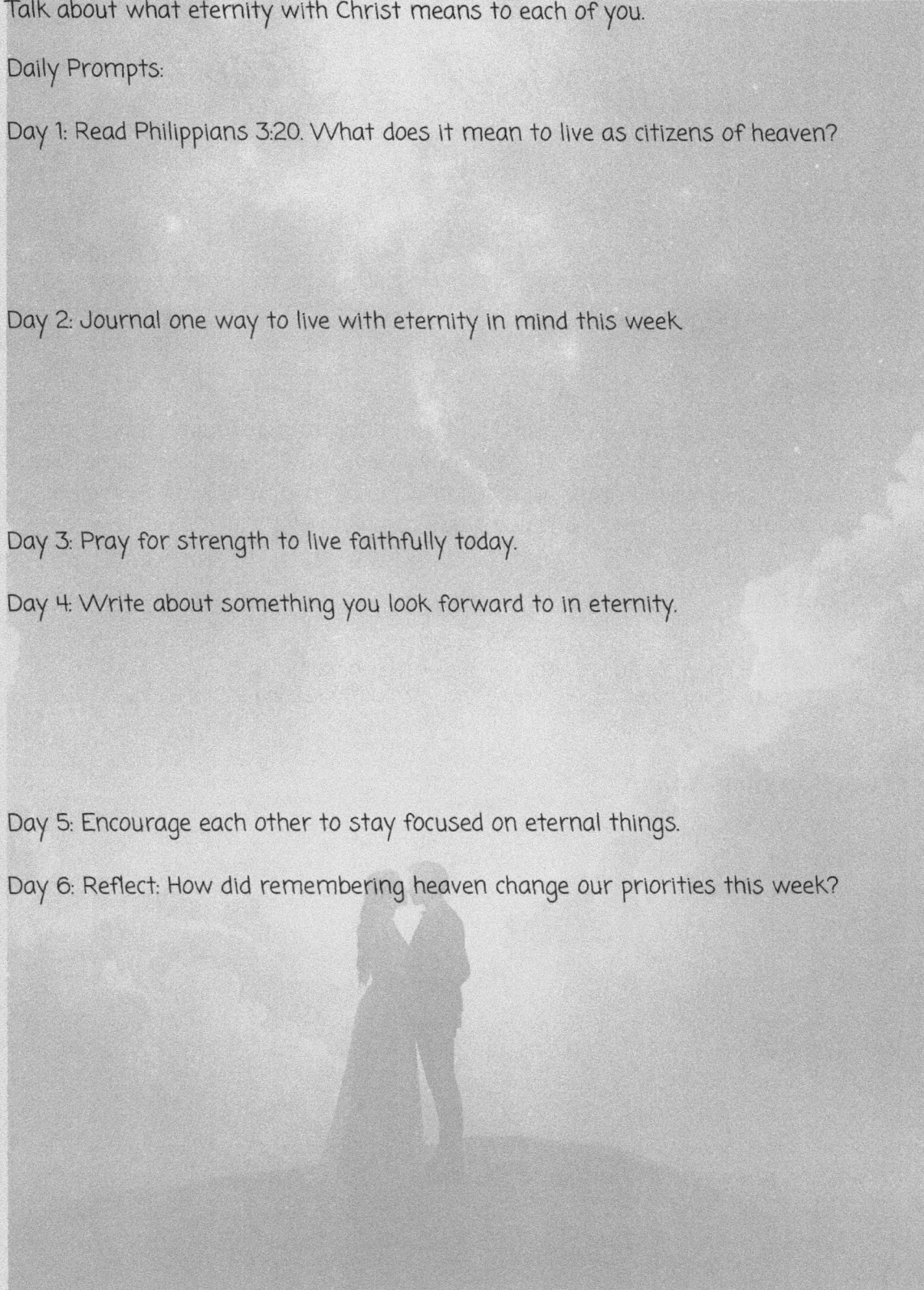

# Finishing the Race Together

## WEEK 50

### SCRIPTURE FOCUS

"I have fought the good fight, I have finished the race, I have kept the faith." — 2 Timothy 4:7

### SHORT LESSON:

Faith is not only about starting strong but finishing strong. Couples must stay faithful to God and to each other through every season of life. Finishing the race means enduring trials, celebrating victories, and keeping faith alive until the very end. When you finish together, you reflect God's covenant love.

### GUIDED PRAYER:

Lord,
Give us strength to finish well. Help us remain faithful to You and to each other. Let our love endure and our faith remain strong until the end.
Amen.

### REFLECTION QUESTIONS:

What does "finishing the race" mean for our relationship?

How can we encourage each other to stay faithful long-term?

What habits keep our faith strong to the end?

## WEEKLY CHALLENGE

Encourage your partner with one Scripture of endurance each day this week.

Daily Prompts:

Day 1: Read 2 Timothy 4:7. What "race" is God calling us to finish well?

Day 2: Journal one area where we need endurance.

Day 3: Pray for faithfulness in our words, actions, and love.

Day 4: Write about someone whose example inspires perseverance. It can be about a famous person if you do not know someone personally.

Day 5: Encourage your partner with a note of gratitude for their faith. Leave it on the coffee maker. Or lunch container.

Day 6: Reflect: How did perseverance bring us closer this week?

Finishing the Race Together

In 2 Timothy 4:7, Paul wrote, "I have fought the good fight, I have finished the race, I have kept the faith."

These words were part of his final message to Timothy — his dear friend and spiritual son. Paul was near the end of his life, imprisoned in Rome, and reflecting on the journey God had led him through. He wasn't boasting about his strength or achievements. He was declaring victory — not because of what he had done, but because of who God had been to him. His words remind us that faith is not a sprint; it's a lifelong race of endurance, trust, and obedience.

### What Paul Meant

"I have fought the good fight."
→ Paul compared his life to a soldier's battle. He faced persecution, rejection, and hardship, but he never gave up. He stood firm in truth and defended the gospel with courage.
"I have finished the race."
→ The "race" represents life's journey — full of challenges and choices. Paul was saying he completed the mission God gave him. He ran with purpose and didn't stop until the end.
"I have kept the faith."
→ Despite suffering and betrayal, Paul stayed faithful to Jesus. He never lost hope or wavered in his belief, showing us what it means to trust God through every season.

### Reflection Prompts
What does "finishing the race" look like in our relationship and in our walk with God?

How can we encourage each other to stay faithful even when life gets difficult?

What spiritual "fight" are we currently facing that requires endurance?

### Practical Ways to Finish Well

Stay focused on the purpose God gave you — don't compare your race to others.
Encourage each other daily with truth and Scripture.
Persevere through challenges together, remembering that every trial builds strength.
Celebrate small victories — faithfulness grows in consistency, not perfection.
Pray regularly for endurance and unity in your relationship.

### A Couple's Prayer
Dear Heavenly Father,
Thank You for the example of Paul, who finished his race with faith and courage.  Help us run our race together with perseverance and purpose.  When we grow weary, remind us that You are our strength.
Keep us faithful, steadfast, and united until the end.  May we finish our race with joy, knowing we have kept the faith.  Amen.

✝ Luke 9:23-24 — Taking Up the Cross Daily

"Then He said to them all: 'Whoever wants to be My disciple must deny themselves and take up their cross daily and follow Me. For whoever wants to save their life will lose it, but whoever loses their life for Me will save it.'"

Meaning:

Jesus makes it clear that following Him isn't about convenience — it's about commitment and surrender. To "take up your cross" means to willingly accept the cost of obedience, even when it's hard, uncomfortable, or misunderstood. True discipleship means dying to selfish desires and choosing God's way every single day.

🌿 Luke 14:27 — Counting the Cost

"And whoever does not carry their cross and follow Me cannot be My disciple."

Meaning:

Following Jesus requires intentional choice — not halfway devotion. It's about giving up anything that competes with Him in your heart. Whether it's pride, comfort, or control, God calls us to lay it down and trust Him completely.

🔥 Romans 12:1 — A Living Sacrifice

"Therefore, I urge you, brothers and sisters, in view of God's mercy, to offer your bodies as a living sacrifice, holy and pleasing to God—this is your true and proper worship."

Meaning:

This verse shows that following God isn't a one-time act, but a daily offering — surrendering your choices, actions, and heart to His will. It's about living in a way that honors Him, even when it means saying no to the world's way.

🌱 Summary Thought

Following God is not always easy — but it always leads to life. Every act of surrender becomes a seed that grows into something greater in His plan. God never wastes a sacrifice; He uses it to draw you closer to His heart.

✝

# A Marriage that Reflects Christ

## WEEK 51

### SCRIPTURE FOCUS

"Husbands, love your wives, just as Christ loved the church and gave himself up for her." — Ephesians 5:25
"Therefore what God has joined together, let no one separate." — Mark 10:9

### SHORT LESSON:

Marriage is a picture of Christ's love for the church. Husbands are called to love sacrificially, and wives to respect and support. Together, they reflect the beauty of the gospel—selfless love, unity, and faithfulness. Couples who live this calling become living testimonies of Christ's love.

### GUIDED PRAYER:

Heavenly Father,
You are the Author of love and the Designer of marriage. From the beginning, You joined man and woman so they would walk in unity, reflect Your image, and reveal Your faithfulness to the world. Teach us to love each other with the same self-giving love Christ showed His church — a love that serves, forgives, and endures. Let our marriage be built on grace rather than perfection, humility rather than pride, and prayer rather than pressure.
When we disagree, remind us that we are not opponents, but one body joined by Your hand. When life feels heavy, help us lean on You and on each other. Guard our covenant from anything that would divide or destroy it, for it is written: "What God has joined together, let no one separate."

In Jesus' Holy Name, Amen

### REFLECTION QUESTIONS:

Does our love reflect Christ's love to the world?

What can I do to show more Christlike love to my partner?

How does our relationship witness to others about Jesus?

## WEEKLY CHALLENGE

Do one act of sacrificial love for your partner each day this week

Daily Prompts

:Day 1: Read Ephesians 5:25. What does Christlike love look like in marriage?

Day 2: Write one way to show sacrificial love this week.

Day 3: Journal a time you saw Christ's character in your partner.

Day 4: Pray for your love to reflect God's grace.

Day 5: Pray and thank God for the covenant of marriage.

Day 6: Reflect: How did loving like Christ change our hearts this week?

# Commitment for Life

## SCRIPTURE FOCUS

"What God has joined together, let no one separate." — Mark 10:9

## SHORT LESSON:

Marriage is a lifelong covenant designed by God. Commitment means choosing love daily, through joy and trial, until the end. Couples who honor their covenant reflect God's faithfulness to the world. True love is not based on feelings but on choice, sacrifice, and obedience.

## GUIDED PRAYER:

Father,
Thank You for uniting us. Help us keep our covenant, staying faithful through every season. Let our love remain strong and unbreakable in You.
Amen.

## REFLECTION QUESTIONS:

Do I view our relationship as a covenant, not just a contract?

What habits help us stay committed for life?

How does God's faithfulness encourage me to stay faithful?

## WEEKLY CHALLENGE

Renew your commitment by praying together over your relationship daily this week

DAILY PROMPTS:

Day 1: Read Mark 10:9. What does "let no one separate" mean to you?

Day 2: Write about how God has strengthened your commitment over time.

Day 3: Pray for lifelong faithfulness and unity.

Day 4: Journal one lesson you've learned this year about love and endurance.

Day 5: Write a renewal promise or prayer for your partner.

Day 6: Reflect: How has God shaped our love into a lifelong covenant?

# God's love—is what holds everything together.

## CLOSING SECTION

### SCRIPTURE FOCUS

"And over all these virtues put on love, which binds them all together in perfect unity."
Colossians 3:14

A Prayer of Commitment
Dear Heavenly Father,
Thank You for walking with us through this journey of 52 weeks. Thank You for the lessons we've learned, the prayers we've shared, and the ways You've drawn us closer to You and to each other. Today, we recommit our relationship into Your hands. Teach us to keep You first in every choice, every word, and every season of life. Help us to love each other with patience, kindness, and faithfulness, just as Christ loves us. May our relationship always reflect Your glory, and may our love be a testimony of Your grace.
In Jesus' name, Amen.

Reflection Questions
Take time together to reflect on your year of growth:
What is one lesson about God that has changed us the most this year?
What is one way our relationship has grown stronger in Christ?
What new habits do we want to continue as we move forward?
What prayer requests has God answered for us over the past year?

A Renewal Challenge
This journal may end, but your journey with God continues.
Keep praying daily as a couple.
Keep opening the Word of God together.
Keep surrounding yourselves with a strong, faith-filled community.
Consider repeating these prompts again next year, or writing your own weekly focus as God continues to teach you.
Let your love be a living testimony of Christ's love to the world.

A Final Blessing
"May the Lord bless you and keep you.
May the Lord make His face shine on you and be gracious to you.
May the Lord turn His face toward you and give you peace."
— Numbers 6:24-26